# THE BIRTH OF CINEMA

## WINGED WORDS AND MOVING PICTURES IN HOMER'S *ILIAD*

## Brett Robbins

APORIA
PRESS

First Aporia Press Edition 2017

ISBN-10: 0-69-282886-9
ISBN-13: 978-0-692-82886-1

Printed in the United States of America

10 9 8 7 6 5 4 3 2 1

**THANKS TO
VINCENT VAN GOGH
AND CHARLIE PARKER**

# CONTENTS

# INTRODUCTION

"What we need is a 'cinematographer's guide' to the classics of literature." (Eisenstein, 1970b: 83)

In his *Poetics*, the cornerstone of modern narratology,[1] Aristotle establishes plot as the most, and spectacle as the least, important of the six elements of tragedy.[2] This initiates a bias for time and against space that continues to shape the narratological agenda to the present day.[3] Lessing, for example, characterizes painting and poetry as fundamentally spatial and temporal art forms, respectively. He argues that, because only pictures can sufficiently represent objects in space, the poet, if he is to realize the potential of his medium, must limit himself to the representation of events in time.[4] Even Joseph Frank's theory of Spatial Form—which, according to James A.W. Heffernan, "breaks through the barrier that Lessing so conspicuously erected between the verbal and visual arts"[5] and which, although it is usually associated with the modern

---

[1] Cf. Chatman (1981a: 259).

[2] 1989: 58, 60. According to Edmunds (1996: 22), this extreme minimization of the role of spectacle in narrative reflects a contemporary debate about the relative importance of playwright and director to the art of tragedy, inducing Aristotle "to try to rescue the text from performance." For more on the narratological bias toward plot, cf. Chatman (1981a: 262); Rimmon-Kenan (1983: 2); Hawkes (1977: 65, 68); Scholes (1974: 59); Gülich/Quasthoff (1985: 173). On the other hand, for a provocative inquiry into the existence of story and discourse as separate entities, and on the question of why we should even bother making this distinction in the first place, cf. Smith (1981: 224-25 and 220-21, respectively).

[3] For more on this narratological "bias" (as Frazier [1999: 468] calls it) toward time, cf. Scholes (1974: 59); Bal (1985: 93); Balutowa (1976: 433, 1979: 7-8); Rimmon-Kenan (1983: 6); Genette (1980: 215); Wiles (1997: 4); Lowe (2000: 41).

[4] 1984: 76. Among Homerists, Becker (1995: 22) takes issue with Lessing, objecting that "the Shield of Achilles...interrupts the narrative to dwell upon objects in space."

[5] 1987b: 63. Cf. also 1987a: 100. For more on the concept of Spatial Form and its congeners, cf. Landow (1987: 77-8), who replies directly to Heffernan; Arnheim (1992: 37); Balutowa (1979: 8); Foucault (1970: 113); Zoran (1984: 311).

1

novel,[6] Oivind Andersen applies to Homeric epic[7]—is really a way to spatialize time rather than to treat space *per se*.[8]

The only book-length treatment of narrative space in Homer to date is Brigitte Hellwig's study, *Raum und Zeit in Homer*.[9] *Raum* in German, however, is ambiguous: It means both "space" and "place."[10] Hellwig emphasizes the latter sense of the word, reducing the wealth of spatial detail in the *Iliad* and *Odyssey* to a finite number of places and charting their trajectory throughout each respective epic. In order to generalize about the kinetic behavior of certain groups of characters she concentrates on the places where *events* of the plot transpire rather than on the spaces where *actions* transpire in individual scenes. She observes, for example, that in the *Iliad* divine activity gradually progresses from Ethiopia to the Trojan plain:

In fünf Etappen nähern sich also die Götter dem Geschehen: Äthiopien--Olymp—Ida und Samothrake—Grabmal des Herakles und "Kallikolone"--Schlachtfeld.[11]

Thus, Hellwig applies to space the structuralist methodology typically devoted to time, extracting from it a hypothetical temporality that subordinates experience to exegesis and disregards all but those spatial phenomena that survive the process of paraphrase.[12]

---

[6] Cf. Poulet, 1977: 106.

[7] 1987: 2.

[8] Cf. Fish (1980b: 83), Zoran (1984: 312). According to Heffernan (1987a: 104), art criticism exhibits the opposite tendency: "The literary critic's tendency to spatialize literature is...mirrored by the art critic's tendency to temporalize art."

[9] Also worth mentioning are Horrocks (1980) and Lateiner (1995), which deal with aspects of space outside the purview of the present work.

[10] For more on the distinction between space and place as distinct narrative categories, cf. Bal (1985: 93); Balutowa (1979: 27); Ronen (1990: 32); Klein (1990: 174); Styan (1988: 196); de Certeau (1984: 117); Zoran (1984: 323).

[11] 1964: 28.

[12] The classic statement of the limitations of paraphrase as a heuristic tool is Brooks' (1974: 196) indictment against the "heresy of paraphrase" and his notion of "the resistance which any good poem sets up against all attempts to paraphrase it." Yet Brooks was anticipated by Longinus (1989: 172). Cf. also Rimmon-Kennan (1983: 8); Fish

There exists, however, an aesthetic dimension of narrative as well, within which actions are conveyed to the audience in real time through the process of *enargeia*[13] before they are abstracted into story-events.[14] Although *enargeia* is all but neglected by narratology,[15] it was considered to be an essential element of Homer's art at least since the scholiasts.[16] Longinus, however, was the first ancient theorist to privilege it as the most potent weapon in the poet's creative arsenal, favoring the ability to "make the speaker *see* what he is saying and bring it *visually* before his audience"[17] over the "ability to order and arrange material."[18]

---

(1980a: 180, 1980b: 89); Shklovsky (1990: 5); Todorov (1981: 4); Cassirer (1946: 37); Greimas (1990: 159).

[13] Cf. Leach (1988: 7): "In the verbal realm, the counterpart of verisimilitude is *enargeia*, or the achievement of persuasively lifelike description....*Enargeia* is directed by the speaker to the spectator. Although its artfulness derives from the speaker's verbal facility, its effects fall short of completion without the spectator's response." For more on the link between *enargeia* and audience, cf. Bakker (1993: 18); Bryant-Bertail (2000: 25); Esslin (1976: 53-4); Gillespie (1988: 103); Tomkins (1980: ix); Iser (1980: 50-51); Werth (1995: 191).

[14] Culler (1986: 82); Todorov (1977c: 55); Scholes (1974: 59).

[15] Regarding the insignificance of purely spatial phenomena according to the traditional narratological model, cf. Barthes, 1989: 141; Todorov, 1977b: 77; Genette, 1980: 165; Lévi-Strauss, 1976: 133; Scholes, 1974: 41; Shklovsky, 1990: 5. That is not to say, however, that temporality and an attention to firsthand narrative experience are necessarily mutually exclusive. Despite the priority he gives to narrative time, for example, Ricoeur (1981: 169) resists the structuralist practice of relegating time to the domain of "events," emphasizing instead the experiential aspects of time as a narrative element, differentiating between "the shift in meaning that distinguishes the 'now' belonging to this time of preoccupation from 'now' in the sense of an abstract instant." In that sense, Ricoeur's temporality partakes in the Longinian *ethos* otherwise associated exclusively with space herein.

[16] Bakker, 1993: 18. Gentili (1988: 5), however, traces this heuristic emphasis on *enargeia* to the fifth-fourth century B.C. poet Simonides of Ceos. Even Aristotle (1989: 72) and Lessing (1984: 85) value *enargeia*, despite its incongruity with their positions toward spectacle and the limitations of the verbal representation of space, respectively. Quintilian also reserves a privileged place for *enargeia* in his rhetorical theory (Leach, 1988: 14-15).

[17] 1989: 159.

[18] Ibid.: 143.

3

As such, Longinus provides a formidable counterpoise to Aristotelian temporocentrism,[19] giving as much priority to the ecstasy generated by the discourse[20] as Aristotle gives to the catharsis generated by the story.[21] Adopting a Longinian perspective on Homeric epic, Paolo Vivante asserts: "Least of all can the Homeric poems be read with a voracious interest in plot and its denouement," preferring instead "to let a thing become an image the moment it is mentioned" and "[to take] Homer's expression at its face value."[22] What distinguishes Vivante's approach to Homer is the emphasis he gives to the *audience's experience* of narrative.

Scholars have traditionally relied upon Homer's representation of the activity of singers within his poems to extrapolate information about his audience and how his art most likely affected them.[23] This approach seeks to understand the singer-audience dynamic by observing fictional singers engaging in an activity similar to that of Homer, with the implicit conviction that the data these fictional representations yield correspond more or less precisely to their real-world referents. To encounter Homeric epic directly, however, it is more useful to observe, not merely the singer's diegetic representation of singers and audiences, but his own

---

[19] Indeed, Lessing (1984: 154) himself acknowledges Longinus as the most formidable rival to Aristotle. In fact, by privileging the spatial aspects of narrative Longinus effects the same sort of synchronic recalibration of the study of narrative as Lévi-Strauss (1963: 34) does for the study of kinship systems. Among modern artists, Artaud (who [1958: 38] advocates "the substitution, for the poetry of language, of a poetry in space which will be resolved in precisely the domain which does not belong strictly to words") "overturns the Aristotelian ranking of the parts of tragedy, putting the spectacle on top (Edmunds, 1996: 15; Cf. also Ibid.: 34-5)." Cf. Bachelard (1964: xviii) and Fish (1980b: 73) for phenomenological and Reader Response perspectives on the priority of space over time, respectively.

[20] 1989:143.

[21] 1984: 67.

[22] 1985: 8, 3, 12, respectively. For cinematic parallels, cf. Osadnik (1994: 225); Münsterberg (1970: 57).

[23] Cf. Carter, 1995: 286; West, 1981: 113.

extradiegetic[24] activity itself and the strategies he employs to integrate his audience into the fabric of the text, as essential collaborators in the production of narrative meaning.[25]

In this study—which makes available to the public, with minor changes, my Indiana University dissertation, *Framing Achilles: Narrative Space in the Iliad*—I offer a narratological reading of Homer's *Iliad* from the standpoint of space rather than, the usual emphasis, time. I establish the frame as the primary link between audience and action and the manipulation of frames as the basis for a dedicated approach to narrative space. I identify cinema theory as the most useful heuristic analogue for coming to terms with the receptive dimension of Homeric space, emphasizing the cognitive links rather than the historical distance between epic and cinema. I demonstrate how Homer employs four proto-cinematic devices in the *Iliad*—decomposition, intercutting, meta-audience, and vignette—to achieve montage-like control over his audience's attention and to reveal a semantic dimension to the epic that manifests itself exclusively through spatial artistry. My intention is not to minimize the significance of the temporal approach to narrative or to Homer in particular, but rather to emphasize that by limiting our focus to the events extrapolated from a direct acquaintance with the narrative—the preoccupation of traditional narratology—we succumb to the illusion that what we say about a story is identical to how we experience it.

---

[24] Cf. Prince (1987): "diegetic. Pertaining to or part of a given diegesis" (20); "diegesis. The fictional world in which the situations and events narrated occur" (20); "extradiegetic. External to (not part of) any diegesis"; cf. Leach (2000: 251).

[25] Cf. Gentili (1988: 22); Rehm (1994: 11).

# CHAPTER ONE

# TYPOLOGY OF HOMERIC SPACE

"Do we have 'space' in Homer?" (Hiller, 82)

## Frame: Pictorial/Verbal

"Homer had no need for graphics; words were all he needed." (Antoniades, 1992: 44)

According to Meyer Schapiro, imagery is conveyed from poet to audience through the medium of the frame, which facilitates communication between them:[26]

The frame belongs then to the space of the observer rather than of the illusory, three-dimensional world disclosed within and behind. It is a finding and focusing device placed between the observer and the image.

In his article, "Image and Frame in Greek Art," Jeffrey Hurwit differentiates between two primary types of artistic frame: closed and open.[27] Hurwit defines the closed frame in the following way:

In closed form the shape given a pictorial field establishes the disposition of elements and axes within the composition, and the border thus guides one's vision toward the dominant internal co-ordinates—the armature—of the image.[28]

As an example of closed composition, Hurwit cites the krater by Exekias that depicts Achilles and Ajax engaged in a game of dice:

---

[26] 1969: 227. Cf. Leach (2000: 237).

[27] 1977: *passim*. For others who adopt the same closed/open framic antinomy, cf. Schapiro (1969: 228); Suvin (1987: 313); Bal (1985: 95-6).

[28] 1977: 1.

He observes how the characters lean over at precisely the point where the vase tapers off on either side, in conformity to the slant of their backs.[29] It is obvious, then, that Exekias tailors the iconography to conform to the vase-shape, resulting in a closed composition that focuses the audience's attention inward, toward the table between the two characters, rather than outward, toward some hypothetical background to the action. It is this centripetal orientation, this gravitation toward the center and subordination of all imagery to this priority, that distinguishes the closed frame from its opposite: the open frame.

Hurwit goes on to define the open frame:

> There is, however, another kind of pleasure...obtained...through the perception of limit transcended, of extension rather than closure, of release rather than confinement. When picture content and the picture space defined by the border or frame do not perfectly coincide, when the relationship between them appears more adventitious than ordered, open form results.[30]

As an example of open composition, Hurwit cites the depiction of the theft of the Arcadian cattle by the Dioscuri:

He notes that the adjacent triglyphs in this metope from the Sikyonian treasury would have overlapped both the hindquarters of the cattle and the protruding spear of the figure to the left. Thus, rather than a sense of

---

[29] Ibid: 1-2.

[30] Ibid: 5, 7.

closure and symmetry, the open frame gives the impression that it encompasses only part of the total action, which the spectator must understand to exist just outside of its borders,[31] lending this type of frame as persistent a sense of centifugality as the centripetality of its closed counterpart.

Because Hurwit limits his purview to static art forms, however, his conception of the frame, whether closed or open, is limited to a single frame encompassing whatever imagery lies within it. This basic frame-scheme has its roots at least as far back as the Bronze Age.[32] The Ship Fresco on the South wall frieze in Room 5 of the West House at Akrotiri, Thera, for example, depicts a fleet of ships framed by two towns inhabited by characters preoccupied by the nautical spectacle between them.[33] As such, the Ship Fresco, like Exekias' krater, constitutes a closed composition, self-contained in its centripetal orientation. It is also possible, however, to embed frames within other frames. In Room 4 of the West House, for example, the artist presents several panels of the interior of a ship

whose exterior is depicted in long shot within the panoramic view of the Ship Fresco:[34]

---

[31] Ibid: 7-8.

[32] Cf. Schapiro, 1969: 224.

[33] Cf. page 16, below.

[34] Cf. Davis, 1991: 6-7.

Granted, this sense of progression from close-up to long shot is only implicitly kinetic, relying upon the spectator to walk from Room 4 to Room 5 to achieve its effect:[35]

Yet the West House frescoes provide evidence of an artist working in a static medium seeking to mobilize its framic structure, to isolate a segment of narrative within the larger, collective frame that encompasses the total action.[36] Indeed, it is the first extant example of the proto-cinematic impulse.

It is worth considering where the West House Painter might have gotten the idea to engage in framic artistry in the first place. Archaeological evidence suggests the existence of a contemporary Late

---

[35] That is not to say that the pictorial use of the close-up is limited to dynamic art forms—it may be used in, for example, single-canvas paintings as well, although in that case diverse framic distances must be used simultaneously, as with certain twentieth-century painters such as Léger (1988: 372).

[36] Vase-painters who seek to incorporate more than a single narrative moment into their compositions also compensate for the inherent staticity of their art form by either combining two or more events within a single frame or by depicting two separate events on separate, often opposite, sections of the vase (Stansbury-O'Donnell, 1999: 156), requiring the spectator to twist the vase to reveal the next event, the vase-painting equivalent of the perambulation required between Rooms 4 and 5 of the West House; cf. Brooks (1974: 203) for a direct comparison between poetic and architectural structure.

Bronze Age poetic tradition.[37] Furthermore, Sarah P. Morris argues that the Miniature Fresco exhibits epic-like themes that reveal continuity between this tradition and Homeric epic.[38] The close-up/long shot transition between Rooms 4 and 5 of the West House corroborates Morris' theory, yet on a stylistic rather than thematic basis. Consider, for example, the following scene from the end of Book 2 of the *Odyssey*:

| | |
|---|---|
| OD.2.414 | οἱ δ' ἄρα πάντα φέροντες ἐυσσέλμῳ ἐνὶ νηὶ |
| OD.2.414 | They all carried the provisions down, and stowed them in the strong-benched |
| OD.2.415 | κάτθεσαν, ὡς ἐκέλευσεν Ὀδυσσῆος φίλος υἱός. |
| OD.2.415 | vessel, in the way the dear son of Odysseus directed them. |
| OD.2.416 | ἂν δ' ἄρα Τηλέμαχος νηὸς βαῖν', ἦρχε δ' Ἀθήνη, |
| OD.2.416 | Telemachos went aboard the ship, but Athene went first |
| OD.2.417 | νηὶ δ' ἐνὶ πρυμνῇ κατ' ἄρ' ἕζετο: ἄγχι δ' ἄρ' αὐτῆς |
| OD.2.417 | and took her place in the stern of the ship, and close beside her |
| OD.2.418 | ἕζετο Τηλέμαχος. τοὶ δὲ πρυμνήσι' ἔλυσαν, |
| OD.2.418 | Telemachos took his place. The men cast off the stern cables |
| OD.2.419 | ἂν δὲ καὶ αὐτοὶ βάντες ἐπὶ κληῖσι καθῖζον. |
| OD.2.419 | and themselves also went aboard and sat to the oarlocks. |
| OD.2.420 | τοῖσιν δ' ἴκμενον οὖρον ἵει γλαυκῶπις Ἀθήνη, |
| OD.2.420 | The goddess gray-eyed Athene sent them a favoring stern wind, |
| OD.2.421 | ἀκραῆ Ζέφυρον, κελάδοντ' ἐπὶ οἴνοπα πόντον. |
| OD.2.421 | strong Zephyros, who murmured over the wine-blue water. |
| OD.2.422 | Τηλέμαχος δ' ἑτάροισιν ἐποτρύνας ἐκέλευσεν |
| OD.2.422 | Telemachos then gave the sign and urged on his companions |
| OD.2.423 | ὅπλων ἅπτεσθαι: τοὶ δ' ὀτρύνοντος ἄκουσαν. |
| OD.2.423 | to lay hold of the tackle, and they listened to his urging |
| OD.2.424 | ἱστὸν δ' εἰλάτινον κοίλης ἔντοσθε μεσόδμης |
| OD.2.424 | and, raising the mast pole made of fir, they set it upright |
| OD.2.425 | στῆσαν ἀείραντες, κατὰ δὲ προτόνοισιν ἔδησαν, |
| OD.2.425 | in the hollow hole in the box, and made it fast with forestays, |
| OD.2.426 | ἕλκον δ' ἱστία λευκὰ ἐυστρέπτοισι βοεῦσιν. |
| OD.2.426 | and with halyards strongly twisted of leather pulled up the white sails. |
| OD.2.427 | ἔπρησεν δ' ἄνεμος μέσον ἱστίον, ἀμφὶ δὲ κῦμα |
| OD.2.427 | The wind blew into the middle of the sail, and at the cutwater |

---

[37] Cf. Bennet (1997: 529); Morris (1989: 511). It is also possible, of course, that the wall-painter provided a model for the epic poet, *pace* Lessing (1984: 62). In either case, the salient fact is that the West House Painter exhibits a proto-cinematic tendency that the epic poet, as we shall see, is able to exploit more fully due to the inherently dynamic nature of his verbal medium.

[38] Morris, 1989: 531.

OD.2.428 στείρη πορφύρεον μεγάλ' ἴαχε νηὸς ἰούσης:
OD.2.428 a blue wave rose and sang strongly as the ship went onward.
OD.2.429 ἡ δ' ἔθεεν κατὰ κῦμα διαπρήσσουσα κέλευθον.
OD.2.429 She ran swiftly, cutting across the swell her pathway.[39]

The two-fold alternation between the interior (414-15, 423-25) and exterior (420-21, 427-29) of the ship provides the verbal equivalent of the pictorial imagery in Rooms 4 and 5. Homer approaches and retreats from the action in the same way as the West House Painter: by isolating a single perspective on a larger scene and then cutting back from it to encompass the scene in its totality. Unlike the West House Painter, however, Homer achieves this effect through words rather than pictures.

According to Rudolf Arnheim, words and pictures exhibit a phenomenological affinity that transcends their superficial differences in media (the foundation of Lessing's negative appraisal of verbal ecphrasis). Arnheim differentiates between two kinds of images: direct and indirect. While direct (or visual) images "come about through the stimulation of the eyes by light generated by or reflected from objects of the physical environment," indirect (or mental) images "are generated by internal stimulation."[40] According to Arnheim, however, even the latter involve a process of mental mediation comparable to that required by words before they can work upon the imagination. He points out that while direct images seem to enjoy a privileged access to immediate experience, they are actually no less subject to mental mediation than so-called indirect images, requiring no less an imaginative effort on our part to perceive them as intelligible contents of whatever artistic continuum they inhere in.[41] From Arnheim's viewpoint, then, verbal imagery is no less suited for the sort of spatial analysis applied to its cinematic

---

[39] All translations of the *Iliad* (Monro, 1902) and *Odyssey* (Goold, 1919) are from Lattimore (1951).

[40] 1987: 83. Chatman (1978: 101) implies that verbal imagery is handicapped, from a communicative standpoint, by its "indirect" status, as Arnheim would call it. Cf. Ibid.: 106.

[41] 1987: 83. Cf. Esrock (1987: 88); Scholes (1982: 25). Even Lessing (1984: 41) acknowledges this fact.

counterpart.[42] In fact, it is more so. Because of its fluid nature, the verbal sign lacks certain limitations to artistic freedom inherent in pictorial media. When, for example, the playwright signifies how far he wishes his audience to imagine itself to be from a given object on stage, this desideratum usually conflicts with the physical reality of the actual distance between them.[43] On the other hand, unlike the wall-painter, vase-painter, playwright, and even filmmaker, Homer has no preformed frame—no wall, vase, stage, or screen—to fill up with dramatic action, but must himself construct this frame, suiting his action to this fundamental choice.[44] In fact, he must construct other frames as well.

By presenting in Room 4 a segment of the all-encompassing action of Room 5, the West House Painter invites us to distinguish between the larger frame and the smaller frame embedded within it, what Seymour

---

[42] Cf., for example, Arnheim's (1987: 85-6) "cinematographic" analysis of Proverbs 7:1-18 of the Book of Proverbs in the King James Version of the Old Testament. Likewise, Leach (1988) seeks to bridge the gap between spectators of visual and literary texts, convinced that the affinities between these diverse media reveal an underlying phenomenological link that warrants such comparative scrutiny. Leach compares the way Homer, Vergil, and the Esquiline Odyssey Painter describe the Laistrygonian harbor that Odysseus enters in Book 10 of the *Odyssey*, concluding that Homer's paratactic style aims for and indeed achieves less scenographic comprehensiveness than the latter two artists (Andersson [1976] shares a similar conviction that Vergil's robust scenographic technique reflects an increased enthusiasm for "topographical coherence." [Leach, 1988: 38]). More salient from the standpoint of reception, however, are the points of convergence Leach sees between the scenographic styles of Vergil and the Esquiline Odyssey Painter despite their distinctive media, as well as her attempt, inspired by this insight, to "...[understand] the imaginative resources for translating words into pictures which Roman audiences could employ to experience description, and conversely, how they might experience pictures by translating them into words." (30) Although Leach's primary focus is on the description of landscape rather than on the space that is created in conjunction with the flow of action—that is to say, specifically *Homeric* space (32)—her inquiry into the phenomenological convergence between pictorial and verbal art forms and their respective audiences, and the centrality of *enargeia* in this connection (7), has equal relevance to this work.

[43] Cf. Edmunds (1996: 32); Lutwack (1984: 13).

[44] Cf. Lutwack (1984: 17-18); Langellier (1981: 115); Balutowa (1979: 14); Klein (1990: 176); Davis (1986-87: 89); Nicolaescu (1988: 60); de Jong (1987: 105-06).

Chatman calls story space and discourse space, respectively,[45] corresponding to the central narratological distinction between story ("the content plane of narrative"[46]) and discourse ("the expression plane of narrative"[47]). The notion of a frame-within-a-frame is coopted in various fields such as semiotics,[48] theater,[49] cinema,[50] and literature proper.[51] Yet Arnheim's formulation, which he applies to fine art yet is equally salient to verbal narrative, epitomizes the profound interdependence between story space and discourse space:[52]

...there are two ways of analyzing pictorial space, both of which are to be considered in all cases. Starting from a composition as a whole, we see a tissue of interwoven units and intervals, all fitting in one unbroken overall system and held together by intrinsic space. When, however, we start from the units, we see sub-systems meeting, crossing, repelling, or paralleling one another, all this taking place in the arena of an extrinsic space system. The meaning of the work requires the apprehension of both structural versions: the nature of the whole and the behavior of its parts.

While story space ("the whole") encompasses the total space of a narrative, discourse space ("its parts") encompasses a particular zone within the story space to which the audience's attention is to be directed.[53] Just as important, however, Arnheim's metaphorical characterization of the "meeting, crossing, repelling, or paralleling" of discourse spaces ("sub-systems") in a painting begs the question of how framing manifests itself in a truly dynamic art form such as epic or cinema. It also suggests that the sort of transition from close-up to long shot depicted in Rooms 4 and 5 only begins to approach the variety of

---

[45] Cf. Chatman (1978: 96).

[46] Prince, 1987: 91.

[47] Ibid.: 21.

[48] Cf. de Certeau (1984: 117-19); Shklovsky (1990: 3).

[49] Cf. Esslin (1976: 46).

[50] Cf. Feldman (1952: 37); Kepley (1995: 98).

[51] Cf. Zoran (1984: 321).

[52] 1966: 67.

[53] To use the example above, Room 4 of the West House presents a discourse-spatial perspective, a close-up view, of the story-spatial totality of the Ship Fresco in Room 5.

kinetic artistry possible within a narrative art work.

Like the West House Painter, Homer exploits the frame-within-the-frame, yet makes extensive use of it over several "rooms" as only the practitioner of a dynamic art form can do, a prerogative which even Lessing acknowledges:

The principal superiority [of the poetic description over the painting] is that the poet leads us to the scene through a whole gallery of paintings, of which the material picture shows only one.[54]

Before we turn to Homer, however, let us enter Room 5 of the West House and see how the artist attempts to compensate for the staticity of his medium through implicit *kinesis*:

Once inside, you stand before a fresco on the North wall (obverse in the picture above) depicting a sea battle and a pastoral scene, representing wartime and peacetime activities:

Then, prompted by the implied westward movement of the fisherman in

---

[54] 1984: 72.

the north-east corner,[55] you walk along the West wall to encounter the South wall frieze, which depicts the aftermath of the sea battle, the homecoming of the warriors:

You recognize the panels of the decorated ship in the middle of this fresco and are thus induced to return imaginatively to where you were in Room 4: inside the ship. You are suddenly the protagonist of an elaborate drama. Yet you are also its primary spectator. As you sail on, you are simultaneously aware of being watched by the occupants of both coasts. Because the fresco cannot be viewed at a single glance, however, you alternate between towns A and B. Finally, you move on: as protagonist, to town B, your diegetic destination; as spectator, to the East wall frieze, your extradiegetic destination:

Suddenly you are in another world, the world of the Elsewhere. Just as the panels of Room 4 induced you to inhabit the ship in Room 5, as well as to see the world through its owner's eyes, now, on the East wall, you are invited to see through his imagination. The world you imagine, however, is not like the world you see with your eyes: it is an exotic world, a land of fantasy, inhabited by mythical creatures occupying an idyllic landscape.[56]

Thus, as the protagonist of the Room 5 narrative, you inhabit its universe, and as a spectator you impart movement to otherwise static images. From Room 4 to 5 you switch from the interior to the exterior of

---

[55] Cf. Marinatos (1984: 51).
[56] Cf. Morris, 1989: 529-30.

a ship. Once inside Room 5 you alternate between towns A and B to witness citizens watching you as you progress to town B. Finally, you travel imaginatively from your immediate surroundings to a distant location. These four types of movement, while distinct in their respective functions for you as both protagonist and spectator, have one thing in common: they require you to actualize them in your own mind, to imagine them as *actually* occurring while in reality they are only implied. This effort on your part is necessary because the pictures on the walls do not really move. The iconography, however, induces you to animate *static* signs *simulating* movement rather than passively to absorb *moving* signs *actualizing* movement, the way Homer, because he employs words rather than pictures, is able to do. We shall now consider how Homer blends story space and discourse space to control his dramatic canvas and, more importantly, the attention of his audience.

## Story Space: Closed/Open

"...an artistic frame indicates an enclosed space, a whole, while a window is only that, a window onto presumably infinite space, a glimpse of just a part." (Frazier, 1999: 453)

Hurwit's distinction between the centripetal and centrifugal orientation of the closed and open frame, respectively, serves as a useful basis by which to differentiate between Iliadic and Odyssean story spaces. The story space of the *Iliad* conforms to Hurwit's closed frame-type. Homer delineates its vertical and horizontal coordinates from the outset, thereby establishing the immutable boundaries within which action will take place for the remainder of the epic,[57] and exhibiting a precise symmetry: Greek camp, Trojan plain, and Troy arranged perpendicularly to Olympus, earth, and Underworld, respectively. Its y (Underworld, Earth, and Olympus)[58] and x (Trojan plain, Greek camp and Troy) axes[59] are

---

[57] Cf. Romm (1992: 10). For cinematic perspectives on this world-building function of the artist, cf. Bazin (1998b: 418); Arnheim (1957: 74-5).
[58] Cf. Wright (1995: 93).

17

introduced metonymically through the imagery of Hades (1.3), dogs and birds (4-5), and Zeus (5), on the one hand, and army (10), ships (12), and Priam (19), on the other. This methodical presentation of Iliadic parameters instills in the audience a permanent sense of groundedness, of conformity to a scenographic master plan that shapes rather than merely accommodates the dramatic activity.[60]

Iliadic story space is dominated by the Trojan plain, representing the main area upon which the action transpires.[61] The Trojan plain is surrounded on all four sides by equally permanent dramatic regions. To the left is the Greek camp,[62] whose topography is presented at length in the Catalogue of Ships in Book 2. To the right is Troy, separated from the plain by the great wall that becomes the focus during the Teixoscopia in Book 3. These two regions constitute the horizontal extremities of the dramatic canvas, its terrestrial limits. Beneath the plain is the Underworld, which receives more dramatic attention in the *Odyssey*. Finally, above the plain is Olympus, home of Zeus and the other Olympian divinities, who constantly watch the action below like spectators in a theatrical audience.[63] This region more than any other characterizes the closed story space of the *Iliad* and determines its centripetal orientation. Homer frequently sets his action in Olympus, providing a god's-eye view[64] on the mortal stage[65] otherwise presented to the audience at ground level. Indeed, while on a diegetic level Iliadic story space assumes cosmic proportions, extradiegetically it resembles an

---

[59] The x, y, and z axes of the three-dimensional Cartesian graph correspond to the horizontal, vertical, and depth dimensions of the spatial continuum, respectively; cf. *Columbia Electronic Encyclopedia* (2003).

[60] Cf. Kuntz (1993: 10).

[61] Cf. Ibid. (9); Hellwig (1964: 24).

[62] Cf. Hainsworth (1993: 189).

[63] Cf. Andersson (1976: 15-16); Griffin (1978: *passim*).

[64] E.g., *Il.* 11.80-83; cf. Richardson (1990: 122-23); Chatman, 1978: 106. Griffin (1978: 1, 5, 11, 14, 15) identifies the Olympians' love of spectatorship as a link between mortal and immortal characters and, by extension, Homer's real-world audience; cf. Leach (1988: 17); Vivante (1985: 5); Richardson (1990: 113).

[65] Cf. Austin (1966: 298); Bakker, (1999: 14); Richardson (1990: 58).

architectural plan of sorts, and in particular that of a palace, consistent with the Homeric conception of the universe as a kind of house, an *imago mundi*.[66] Despite the fact that Olympus and the Underworld are diegetically much further apart than the Greek camp and Troy, the palace-like structure of Iliadic story space fosters the illusion that, on a phenomenological level, these four regions are equidistant from the Trojan plain rather than dispersed over an *Odyssey*-like series of *ad hoc* stages.[67]

The story space of the *Odyssey* is more complex than its Iliadic counterpart. It is useful to distinguish between two kinds of Odyssean scenes: those that transpire inside, and those outside, palatial settings. In the latter case Odyssean story space is diametrically opposite to that of the *Iliad*, conforming to Hurwit's conception of the open frame. It serves, therefore, not as a strictly demarcated container for dramatic action, but rather as an open-ended scenographic field allowing for infinite variety and the freedom to alter along with the action and to contribute to the development of the plot. When Homer shifts the action to Odysseus' palace in Book 17, however, the story space is suddenly no less monolithic than the Iliadic cosmos. Yet there is one major difference: Odysseus' *oikos* constitutes, not merely a literal palace, but the domestic counterpart to and mirror-image of the Iliadic palatial cosmos. Whereas in the *Iliad* the diegetically distant coordinates of the cosmos are presented as extradiegetically proximate, the diegetically proximate coordinates of the Odyssean palace are presented as extradiegetically distant. When, for example, Penelope sits outside of her bedroom—the domestic equivalent to Olympus, with a similar vertical orientation and spectatorial function[68]—she is privy to the goings-on within the

---

[66] Cf. Wright (1995: 18). On the concept of the *imago mundi*, cf. Eliade (1959: 42). According to Paul Demont and Anne Lebeau, palaces functioned as sites for theater-like activity as far back as the Late Bronze Age (1996: 10), and John Bennet entertains the possibility that Homeric epic was itself originally performed within a palatial venue (1997: 529).

[67] Cf. Bassett (1938: 51-2).

[68] E.g., *Od.* 1.328-29, 4.121, 19.89.

megaron, the palatial stage:

OD.20.387 ἡ δὲ κατ' ἄντηστιν θεμένη περικαλλέα δίφρον
OD.20.387 She, Icarius' daughter, prudent Penelope,
OD.20.388 κούρη Ἰκαρίοιο, περίφρων Πηνελόπεια,
OD.20.388 placed a gorgeous chair opposite the door
OD.20.389 ἀνδρῶν ἐν μεγάροισιν ἑκάστου μῦθον ἄκουε.
OD.20.389 and heard the words of each man in the hall.

When, however, she enters her bedroom and closes the door behind her, she is oblivious to the world outside, as far away from the suitors as the Olympian gods are close to the Trojan plain in the *Iliad*. In lines 35-8 in Book 23, for example, she refers to Odysseus' οἶκος as though it were far away rather than where she is currently located, and asks Eurykleia for a report of his whereabouts rather than open her bedroom door and look into the megaron herself.

OD.23.35 εἰ δ' ἄγε δή μοι, μαῖα φίλη, νημερτὲς ἐνίσπες,
OD.23.35 Come, dear nurse, and give me a true account of the matter,
OD.23.36 εἰ ἐτεὸν δὴ οἶκον ἱκάνεται, ὡς ἀγορεύεις,
OD.23.36 whether he really has come back to his house, as you tell me,
OD.23.37 ὅππως δὴ μνηστῆρσιν ἀναιδέσι χεῖρας ἐφῆκε
OD.23.37 to lay his hands on the shameless suitors, though he was only
OD.23.38 μοῦνος ἐών, οἱ δ' αἰὲν ἀολλέες ἔνδον ἔμιμνον.
OD.23.38 one, and they were always lying in wait, in a body!'[69]

This vast metaphorical distance between megaron and bedroom is corroborated in Book 23 when Odysseus refers to his bed the way people in the *Iliad* talk about far away places:[70]

OD.23.202 οὐδέ τι οἶδα,
OD.23.202 I do not know now,

---

[69] ἐνέπω is the same verb used by the narrator to ask the Muse to reveal the identity of the best of the Achaeans in the Catalogue of Ships (2.761), and thus, by its impersonal tone, emphasizes the isolation of Penelope's bedroom from the rest of Odysseus' palace.

[70] Cf. the simile in lines 233-40, which portrays their shared intimate knowledge of the bed as a kind of mystery religion, located on an island across distant waters and accessible only to the initiated.

OD.23.203 εἴ μοι ἔτ' ἔμπεδόν ἐστι, γύναι, λέχος, ἠέ τις ἤδη
OD.23.203 dear lady, whether my bed is still in place, or if some man
OD.23.204 ἀνδρῶν ἄλλοωσε θῆκε, ταμὼν ὕπο πυθμέν' ἐλαίης.
OD.23.204 has cut underneath the stump of the olive, and moved it elsewhere.'

Thus, whereas Homer contracts Iliadic distances to facilitate divine/human interaction, he expands Odyssean distances, and in particular that between Penelope upstairs and Odysseus downstairs,[71] to create the impression of distinct fictional worlds within a single dramatic milieu. Even when characters interact within close proximity of each other, in the Odyssean universe they are still somehow liable to be out of earshot of each other, contrasting markedly with the frequent eavesdropping by the gods from Olympus in the *Iliad*:

OD.2.321 ἦ ῥα, καὶ ἐκ χειρὸς χεῖρα σπάσατ' Ἀντινόοιο
OD.2.321 He spoke, and lightly drew away his hand from Antinoös'
OD.2.322 ῥεῖα: μνηστῆρες δὲ δόμον κάτα δαῖτα πένοντο.
OD.2.322 hand, but the suitors about the house prepared their dinner,
OD.2.323 οἱ δ' ἐπελώβευον καὶ ἐκερτόμεον ἐπέεσσιν.
OD.2.323 and in their conversation they insulted him and mocked him,

By distorting narrative space in this intertextual manner,[72] Homer in effect creates a palace out of a universe and a universe out of a palace to attain correspondingly distinctive stylistic and thematic results in the *Iliad* and the *Odyssey*, respectively.[73]

---

[71] Cf. 20.387-89: the threshold to the bedroom symbolizes this vast gulf between the eavesdroppable here and the otherworldly there.

[72] The spatial intertextuality between the *Iliad* and *Odyssey* extends much further than this, but is outside the purview of this work.

[73] This tendency to contrast closed and open story spaces in two interdependent narratives is echoed cinematically, for example, in the two "Godfather" films, whose scenographic differences, and their dramatic ramifications, are characterized by James Berardinelli (1994).

# Discourse Space: Montage/Realism

"As opposed to Griffith and Eisenstein, filmmakers of the cut, Murnau has usually been thought to be a filmmaker of the moving camera." (Perez, 1998: 132)

In his comparison between the *Iliad* and the *Odyssey*, T.M. Andersson observes:

...the *Iliad* is remarkable among epics because it foregoes the variety afforded by changes of scenery.

He qualifies his statement, however, with the following admission:

Yet the action is not uniform or dull. Homer makes abundant use of movement and tension, which on the whole provide greater narrative energy than the scenic variations of the *Odyssey*.

He goes on to describe what he means by "movement":

The movement is confined to a limited space, but within that space it is more or less constant. There is a perpetual coming and going, an ebb and flow of action across the plain; if one side is not retreating, it is pursuing. This flux is by no means aimless, but takes place within fixed emotional and spatial parameters marked at either extremity by the always imminent threat of total rout on one side or the other.[74]

Thus, Andersson defines Iliadic movement from the point of view of the *characters*. *They* move back and forth on the battlefield. *Their* movement inheres within story space, which "contains existents,"[75] and which Schapiro refers to as "the illusory, three-dimensional world disclosed within and behind [the observer]."[76] Andersson goes on to describe what he means by "tension":

The alternation of panic and desperate rally keeps the reader on edge not because the

---

[74] 1976: 27.

[75] Chatman, 1978: 96.

[76] 1969: 227.

movement itself is exciting but because it maintains the emotions of the contending warriors at fever pitch."[77]

As with movement, Andersson attributes Iliadic tension to the audience's empathy with the characters: we are "on edge" because their "emotions" excite us in a way that the movement itself cannot do. One wonders, however, whether the "movement and tension" Andersson speaks of is really such a worthy substitute for, let alone a greater source of "dramatic energy" than, "the scenic variations of the *Odyssey*," which, after all, involve Odysseus in a compelling series of adventures in their own right and generate their share of "panic and desperat[ion]." On the contrary, I submit that it is not movement and tension within *story space* that produce the distinctive "dramatic energy" of the *Iliad*, but rather movement and tension within *discourse space*, which Chatman defines as:

*...focus of spatial attention...*the framed area to which the implied audience's attention is directed by the discourse, that portion of the total story-space that is "remarked" or closed in upon, according to the requirements of the medium, through a narrator or through the camera eye—literally, as in film, or figuratively, as in verbal narrative.[78]

Discourse space serves as the medium by which the poet produces movement and tension, not between characters, but *within the mind of the audience*. To encounter discourse space we require an alternative paradigm to traditional narratology,[79] one that privileges rather than merely accommodates the experience of the audience in the act of watching the spectacle before them.

---

[77] 1976: 27.

[78] 1978: 102.

[79] An appeal to reception theory (cf. Tomkins, 1980: *passim*) proves relatively fruitless. The mental activity reception theorists are primarily concerned with is concretization, the filling of gaps left by the author, privileging "the fluidity...of the meaning experience" (Fish, 1980: 83) and "the unwritten part [of the text] that gives us the opportunity to picture things" (Iser, 1980: 58). This approach would be more suited to a dedicated study of narrative space in the *Odyssey*, which leaves more room for subjective activity on the audience's part than in the *Iliad*.

The first cinema theorists sought to distinguish their art form from those that preceded it, especially theater.[80] This induced them to emphasize certain devices ostensibly unique to cinema, arguing that the camera, editing, and other technological advances provided them with unprecedented freedom to manipulate space and time and thus to exert psychological effects on their audience impossible to achieve through any other medium.[81] According to Eisenstein, however, these supposedly unique cinematographic features actually derive from literature, which commands an equally comprehensive control over the audience's attention as cinema does, only verbally rather than pictorially.[82] Although Eisenstein limits his examples to the modern novel, he mentions the Greeks as a formative influence on the proto-cinematic techniques employed by Dickens, his primary exemplar[83] of the debt cinema owes to verbal narrative.[84] Furthermore, in the field of narratology, Chatman adopts a comparative approach to literature and cinema, treating the two art forms interchangeably to identify the underlying narrative structures shared between them.[85]

Among Homerists, Mark Edwards attributes to Homer the use of cinema-like devices such as the long shot[86] and meta-audience,[87] and Scott Richardson puts a "camera"[88] in his hands and calls what he does "filming."[89] Despite this avowed affinity between Homer and the filmmaker, however, no one has subjected Homeric epic to a systematic

---

[80] Cf. Pudovkin (1960: 27); Panofsky (1998: 281); Münsterberg (1970: 16); Bazin (1967: 77); Goffman (1974: 144).

[81] Cf. Arnheim (1957: 88); Feldman (1952: 77, 98); Stern (1979: 59, 65); Münsterberg (1970: 45).

[82] 1970b, 1977: *passim.* Cf. Chatman (1978: 105); Pudovkin (1960: 23).

[83] Eisenstein (1970b: 79) also identifies : "several purely cinematic elements in the plastic side of [Emile Zola's] creative work."

[84] 1977: 232. Cf. Zweig (1930: 52).

[85] 1978, 1981b: *passim.*

[86] 1987: 87.

[87] Ibid.: 84.

[88] 1990: 110, 121.

[89] Ibid.: 119.

analysis of what one might be tempted to think of as its proto-cinematic aspects but which, for reasons that will become clear, I prefer to think of as its cinematic aspects per se, underscoring the fact that film is not synonymous with cinema but merely a relatively late manifestation of it. Film is a modern art form, invented roughly three thousand years after Homeric cinema. The confusion of film with cinema proper has led, *inter alios*, Caroline Eades and Françoise Létoublon, who attest to the cinema-like "rhetorical, narrative, and stylistic devices and structures" in Homer, to insist that, on the other hand, to attribute to him the use of "cinematic codes" would be anachronistic, as though the former constituted a category separate from, rather than dependent upon, the latter.[90] Yet when we watch a movie sequence that presents a long shot of a scene, then cuts to a medium shot of a character within that scene, and finally a close-up or extreme close-up of a certain aspect of that character, the effect on the viewer is similar to when the same relative distances are represented in a text.[91] Thus, if this series of shots warrants serious attention as a distinctive stylistic device in cinema, there is no reason why its verbal counterpart, and other proto-cinematic devices, should not also be so honored.[92]

André Bazin differentiates between two primary cinematic styles: montage and realism,[93] corresponding to "those directors who put their faith in the image and those who put their faith in reality,"[94] respectively. Through realism, the filmmaker tends to maintain a consistent distance between audience and action and simply to record the action of the characters, leaving it to the audience, like theatergoers,[95] to direct their attention anywhere within the frame they wish and to give free reign to

---

[90] 1999: 302. Cf. Martin (1986: 144).

[91] Cf. Edwards (1987: 87).

[92] Cf. Bassi (1998: 5), who bases her characterization of Homer as "pre-theatrical" on a kindred appeal to the phenomenological affinities between epic and theater.

[93] 1998: *passim*.

[94] Ibid.: 43.

[95] Cf. Lowe (2000: 163-64). It was this inherent staticity of theater that early filmmakers rejected in favor of the moving camera and editing; cf. Kauffmann (1974: 67-8).

25

their powers of selective perception:[96]

In this case "the image is evaluated not according to what it adds to reality but what it reveals of it,"[97] a quality that Roger Ebert attributes to the movie "The Dancer Upstairs":[98]

"The Dancer Upstairs" is elegantly, even languorously, photographed by Jose Luis Alcaine, who doesn't punch into things but regards them, so that we are invited to think about them.

The realist filmmaker may also pan from place to place, dictating the audience's response to a certain extent, yet preserving the natural flow of time between events and thus maintaining a theater-like sense of lived experience:[99]

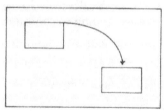

Ebert identifies this tendency in the movie "Elephant":[100]

---

[96] Cf. Esslin (1976: 79). Benjamin (1968: 238) points out the similarity between theater and painting in this regard; cf. Bazin (1998a: 54); Esslin (1976: 81).

[97] Bazin, 1998a: 47. Cf. Arnheim (1957: 76).

[98] 2003a.

[99] Cf. Lotman (1976: 82).

[100] 2003b. Bazin (1998a) characterizes Murnau (46) and Renoir (55) as practitioners of realist cinema: "[Renoir] forced himself to look back beyond the resources provided by montage and so uncovered the secret of a film form that would permit everything to be

The movie is told mostly in long tracking shots; by avoiding cuts between closeups and medium shots, Van Sant also avoids the film grammar that goes along with such cuts, and so his visual strategy doesn't load the dice or try to tell us anything. It simply watches.

Through montage, on the other hand, the filmmaker tends to cut rather than pan between distinct regions of a given location, or even between locations that are far removed in space and time, employing "a whole arsenal of means whereby to impose its interpretation of an event on the spectator":[101]

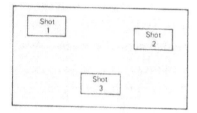

This adds a stylistic dimension to a film that is not inherent in the subject matter and that most significantly distinguishes cinema from theater.[102] At its best, montage complements rather than detracts from its subject matter. A.O. Scott praises this aspect of M. Night Shyamalan's art in his review of the film "Signs":[103]

Mr. Shyamalan is a master of control, with a sure grasp of the classical filmmaking lexicon. His suspense sequences build slowly and elegantly, and he is adept at evoking dread through shifting camera angles and careful manipulation of the frame.

On the other hand, a reviewer at Internet Movie Database expresses

---

said without chopping the world up into little fragments, that would reveal the hidden meanings in people and things without disturbing the unity natural to them."
[101] Bazin, 1998a: 46.
[102] Regarding the manipulation of focal distances, cf. Pichel (1970: 114); Münsterberg (1970: 15-16); Bobker (1974: 47). Regarding the manipulation of space and time, cf. Stansbury-O'Donnell (1999: 412); Arnheim (1957: 89); Feldman (1952: 60-1); Münsterberg (1970: 74); Pudovkin (1960, 83-90).
[103] 2002.

disfavor with the way he believes the film "SLC Punk!" abuses the prerogatives of framic *kinesis*:[104]

There were a few times where the filming absolutely drove me insane...The way it was filmed was just awful, there was (*sic*) way too many film cuts that shouldn't have been there. I can't figure out what kind of effect the director was trying to get there, but it just angered me. I don't think it's a good idea if you're paying more attention to the editing than the dialog that's being said.

The Bazin paradigm provides a useful heuristic model by which to differentiate between discourse space in the *Iliad* and the *Odyssey*. The *Odyssey* adopts a realistic style, maintaining long shot distance from the action and allowing the interaction between characters to move the story along rather than transporting the audience into the scene through medium or close-up shots. In the following passage, for example, Nestor, his sons, and Telamachus enter the stage one after the other:

OD.3.411   Νέστωρ αὖ τότ' ἐφῖζε Γερήνιος, οὖρος Ἀχαιῶν,
OD.3.411   Gerenian Nestor, the Achaians' watcher,
OD.3.412   σκῆπτρον ἔχων. περὶ δ' υἷες ἀολλέες ἠγερέθοντο
OD.3.412   sat there holding his staff, and his sons coming out of their chambers
OD.3.413   ἐκ θαλάμων ἐλθόντες, Ἐχέφρων τε Στρατίος τε
OD.3.413   gathered in a cluster about him, Echephron and Stratios,
OD.3.414   Περσεύς τ' Ἀρητός τε καὶ ἀντίθεος Θρασυμήδης.
OD.3.414   Perseus and Aretos and Thrasymedes the godlike,
OD.3.415   τοῖσι δ' ἔπειθ' ἕκτος Πεισίστρατος ἤλυθεν ἥρως,
OD.3.415   and sixth was the hero Peisistratos who came to join them.
OD.3.416   πὰρ δ' ἄρα Τηλέμαχον θεοείκελον εἶσαν ἄγοντες.
OD.3.416   They brought out godlike Telemachos and seated him next them,
OD.3.417   τοῖσι δὲ μύθων ἦρχε Γερήνιος ἱππότα Νέστωρ:
OD.3.417   and Nestor the Gerenian horseman began speaking to them:

Each character suddenly appears as though he has been waiting in the wings,[105] consistent with the open story space of the *Odyssey*, which rarely seems to contain the action completely but rather, like a window,

---

[104] Cortex, 2002. Cf. Kauffmann (1974: 70).
[105] Regarding the conflation of theatrical and cinematic metaphors, cf. Lowe (2000: 163-64).

to frame it arbitrarily, leaving us uncertain as to what will materialize next. As Hurwit puts it:

The image set "within" the border [of an open frame] seems abbreviated, incomplete, severed....The visual effect of such representations...is to create a porthole through which one views only a portion of a long procession of figures seemingly marching on the other side of the tondo's decorative wall....presents a transient, passing show whose extent is not fully captured by the border."[106]

When the camera does move in the *Odyssey*,[107] it tends to pan between contiguous portions of story space rather than to cut between disparate discourse spaces,[108]

OD.1.143   κῆρυξ δ' αὐτοῖσιν θάμ' ἐπῴχετο οἰνοχοεύων.
OD.1.143   and a herald, going back and forth, poured the wine for them.

preserving the natural flow of time and leaving open "the points of interval that are the inevitable concomitant of every natural event."[109]

Homer frequently lets the audience fill in these gaps themselves. In the following passage, for example, προσηύδα in line 507 presupposes that Penelope has not merely called (καλέσασα) Eumaios but that he has also come within earshot of her before she speaks:

OD.17.505   ἡ μὲν ἄρ' ὣς ἀγόρευε μετὰ δμῳῇσι γυναιξίν,
OD.17.505   So Penelope, sitting up in her chamber, conversed

---

[106] 1977: 6. Cf. Lowe (2000: 164).

[107] Regarding the theoretical basis for the "anachronistic" use of cinematic terms to describe cinema-like phenomena in verbal narrative, cf. Chatman (1978: 105); Landow (1987: 77-8); Richardson (1990), who refers to Homer's "camera."

[108] That is not to say, however, that Homer does not also employ panning in the *Iliad*, even in such a way as to produce a temporary sense of framic openendedness, as when the camera darts temporarily offstage to follow the trajectory of Paris' helmet thrown by Menelaos (3.377) or Imbrios' head thrown by Ajax (13.202-05). Likewise, the *Odyssey* is not entirely devoid of *Iliad*-like cutting (e.g. *Od.* 18.394-400). What is at issue, however, is the *preponderance* of realistic and montagistic tendencies in the two epics, respectively.

[109] Pudovkin, 1960: 90. Cf. Ibid. (83).

OD.17.506 ἠμένη ἐν θαλάμῳ· ὁ δ' ἐδείπνει δῖος Ὀδυσσεύς·
OD.17.506 with her serving women, while great Odysseus was eating his dinner.
OD.17.507 ἡ δ' ἐπὶ οἷ καλέσασα προσηύδα δῖον ὑφορβόν·
OD.17.507 But now she summoned the noble swineherd to her, saying:

Sometimes, however, Homer himself occupies the implied interval between the first and last stages of an action with interstitial material. In Book 1, for example, Eurykleia carries a torch for Telemachus to illuminate the path to his bedroom. Homer represents the time it takes for the two characters to reach their goal, between the first and second use of the phrase ἅμ' αἰθομένας δαΐδας φέρε (428-34), with biographical information about Eurykleia:[110]

OD.1.427 ἔνθ' ἔβη εἰς εὐνὴν πολλὰ φρεσὶ μερμηρίζων.
OD.1.427 He went to bed, and in his mind he pondered many things.
OD.1.428 τῷ δ' ἄρ' ἅμ' αἰθομένας δαΐδας φέρε κέδν' εἰδυῖα
OD.1.428 Devoted Eurycleia, daughter of Ops Peisenorides,
OD.1.429 Εὐρύκλει', Ὦπος θυγάτηρ Πεισηνορίδαο,
OD.1.429 carried burning torches by his side.
OD.1.430 τήν ποτε Λαέρτης πρίατο κτεάτεσσιν ἑοῖσι
OD.1.430 Laertes had bought her with his own possessions once upon a time,
OD.1.431 πρωθήβην ἔτ' ἐοῦσαν, ἐεικοσάβοια δ' ἔδωκεν,
OD.1.431 when she was still in the bloom of youth. He'd given twenty oxen,
OD.1.432 ἶσα δέ μιν κεδνῇ ἀλόχῳ τίεν ἐν μεγάροισιν,
OD.1.432 and in his palace valued her as equal to his devoted wife,
OD.1.433 εὐνῇ δ' οὔ ποτ' ἔμικτο, χόλον δ' ἀλέεινε γυναικός·
OD.1.433 but he avoided his wife's anger and never took her to bed.
OD.1.434 ἥ οἱ ἅμ' αἰθομένας δαΐδας φέρε, καί ἑ μάλιστα
OD.1.434 She carried burning torches by his side. Of the bondswomen,

While the *Iliad* and *Odyssey* are both proto-cinematic from the standpoint of the Bazin paradigm, the *Iliad* lends itself more than the *Odyssey* to a dedicated study of narrative space, for it is montage rather than realism that achieves "the creation of a sense or meaning not proper to the images themselves but derived exclusively from their

---

[110] Cf. also *Od.* 1.428-34, 2.389-407, 3.360-65, 18.77-88, 90-4, and 153-56. Although these passages do not repeat the initial action verbatim as in the present case, they exploit the panning aesthetic in a similar manner.

juxtaposition,"[111] and only the manipulation of frames can achieve "the needed shifting of attention"[112] that Münsterberg attributes to the cinema, but that applies equally well to the *Iliad*.[113] In his article, *"The Birth of a Nation*: The Technique and Its Influence," Seymour Stern identifies Griffith as the chief architect of cinematic montage:

> By crystallizing the basic principles of film technique, which Griffith himself created or discovered, *The Birth of a Nation* gave birth to the film as an art....The study of usages of movement and movement-forms on the screen could be almost completed from an examination of this one film."[114]

Long before Griffith, however, there was Homer.

In the remaining chapters we shall consider four spatial devices that Homer employs in the *Iliad* to achieve with words what the painter simulates through *stasis* and the film director actualizes through *kinesis*: "absolute control over the movements in his film."[115] Each device involves the audience in a different relationship to the action and corresponds to one of the four types of movement adumbrated by the West House Painter. Decomposition (Chapter 2) provides access to the z axis of the spatial continuum through a series of progressively narrowing discourse spaces (long shot, medium shot, close-up), corresponding to

---

[111] Bazin, 1998a: 44.

[112] 1970: 33.

[113] On this priority in cinema, cf. Münsterberg (1970); Bobker (1974: 46). Although the *Iliad* is more montagistic than realistic, it also exhibits realistic tendencies. When, for example, Chryses walks along the beach in Book 1 and prays to Apollo (*Il.* 1.33-6), we see him do so from a consistently distant vantage-point; the meaning of the scene is generated solely by Chryses' actions. The camera does not, for example, cut to his face, revealing tears in his eyes and thus heightening the emotional impact of the scene through extradiegetic means (for more on this scene, cf. pp. 129-31, below). Rather than invalidate the characterization of the *Iliad* as montagistic rather than realistic, however, this scene merely illustrates that some degree of stylistic overlap is possible between the two epics. This is true in cinema as well; cf. Youngblood (2001): "Antonioni is known for the detheatralization of cinema--yet he uses certain theater-like techniques."

[114] 1979: 59, 63.

[115] Feldman, 1959: 124.

the transition from close-up to long shot of the ship in Rooms 4 and 5, respectively. Intercutting (Chapter 3) keeps the audience at long shot range from the action and cuts between the Greek and Trojan zones of Iliadic story space. This corresponds to the visual alternation between towns A and B required by the spectator of the South wall frieze to acknowledge each group of meta-spectators. Both meta-audience (Chapter 4) and vignette (Chapter 5) transport the audience into the mind of a given character. Whereas the former (corresponding to the meta-spectatorship of both the protagonist *from* the ship and the inhabitants of towns A and B *of* the ship) presents the action through the character's *vision*, the latter (corresponding to the protagonist's visualization of the parallel world depicted on the East wall frieze) presents the action through the character's *imagination*.

One might suspect that the montagistic style of the *Iliad* merely reflects its military subject matter, requiring vivid close-ups of battlefield carnage and the sort of parallel action that Griffith canonized cinematically in "The Birth of a Nation":

...the conjoining of two complementary but opposite movements, seen at a tangent to each other...to create a sense of unleashed activity from all directions in...pursuit...and to step up the tempo of imminent violence."[116]

Military subject matter, however, does not determine the presentational itinerary of a given epic; one can treat it in the montagistic style of the *Iliad* or in the realistic style of the *Odyssey*. This is equally true in cinema, as Ebert's review of "Patton" makes clear:

...'Patton' is one of the most uncluttered of war movies...the battle scenes are seen in long shot, not personalized; they have the sweep of Victorian canvases instead of the hand-to-hand intimacy of "Platoon," "Saving Private Ryan" or "We Were Soldiers."[117]

In fact, Homer's use of decomposition, intercutting, meta-audience, and

---

[116] Stern, 1979: 64.
[117] 2002.

vignette is not limited to the military scenes of the *Iliad*. In similes, for instance, the devices may be utilized in contexts unrelated to battle. In Book 24, for example, Iris obeys Zeus' order to find Thetis in her maritime abode and to convince her to visit Zeus in Olympus. Her journey is compared to the trajectory of an ox-horn fishing-line:

IL.24.80  ἣ δὲ μολυβδαίνῃ ἰκέλη ἐς βυσσὸν ὄρουσεν,
IL.24.80  She plummeted to the sea floor like a lead weight which, mounted
IL.24.81  ἥ τε κατ' ἀγραύλοιο βοὸς κέρας ἐμβεβαυῖα
IL.24.81  along the horn of an ox who ranges the fields, goes downward
IL.24.82  ἔρχεται ὠμηστῇσιν ἐπ' ἰχθύσι κῆρα φέρουσα.
IL.24.82  and takes death with it to the raw-ravening fish.

While the simile does not specifically shift from long shot to close-up ranges, it depicts the sort of activity that, when it receives first-order dramatic treatment, lends itself to decomposition. And in the following simile, Homer represents through intercutting the activity of farmers rather than soldiers:

IL.11.67  οἳ δ', ὥς τ' ἀμητῆρες ἐναντίοι ἀλλήλοισιν
IL.11.67  And the men, like two lines of reapers who, facing each other,
IL.11.68  ὄγμον ἐλαύνωσιν ἀνδρὸς μάκαρος κατ' ἄρουραν
IL.11.68  drive their course all down the field of wheat or of barley
IL.11.69  πυρῶν ἢ κριθῶν: τὰ δὲ δράγματα ταρφέα πίπτει:
IL.11.69  for a man blessed in substance, and the cut swathes drop showering,
IL.11.70  ὣς Τρῶες καὶ Ἀχαιοὶ ἐπ' ἀλλήλοισι θορόντες
IL.11.70  so Trojans and Achaians driving in against one another
IL.11.71  δῄουν, οὐδ' ἕτεροι μνώοντ' ὀλοοῖο φόβοιο.
IL.11.71  cut men down, nor did either side think of disastrous panic.

As with the decompositional simile, the actual cutting from side to side is not specified. The phrase ἐναντίοι ἀλλήλοισιν (67), however, implies that if the scene were to be presented fully it would indeed be done so through intercutting.

Meta-audience and vignette, on the other hand, transport the audience immediately into a given character's skin, and thus preclude the gradual progression from long shot to close-up or from arrow-shot to sword-stab ranges required for decomposition and intercutting, respectively. When Agamemon reviews his troops in Book 4, for example, he encounters the two Aiantes, who are surrounded by a "cloud of foot-soldiers":

IL.4.272  Ἀτρείδης δὲ παρῴχετο γηθόσυνος κῆρ:
IL.4.272  Atreides, cheerful at heart, went onward.
IL.4.273  ἦλθε δ' ἐπ' Αἰάντεσσι κιὼν ἀνὰ οὐλαμὸν ἀνδρῶν:
IL.4.273  On his way through the thronging men he came to the Aiantes.
IL.4.274  τὼ δὲ κορυσσέσθην, ἅμα δὲ νέφος εἵπετο πεζῶν.
IL.4.274  These were armed, and about them went a cloud of foot-soldiers.

While this metaphor sufficiently expresses the magnitude of its referent, Homer's emphasis is more on the effect that it has on Agamemnon (and, by extension, on his audience) than on the phenomenon itself. To convey this emotion, however, requires more than what what a mere statement of this fact could provide. Agamemnon's response to seeing these troops is an event, and requires a dramatic comparandum to encompass in more than a merely generic way. Homer achieves this through simile. He compares Agamemnon's experience to what a goatherd feels when he ascertains the signs of an impending storm:

IL.4.275  ὡς δ' ὅτ' ἀπὸ σκοπιῆς εἶδεν νέφος αἰπόλος ἀνὴρ
IL.4.275  As from his watching place a goatherd watches a cloud move
IL.4.276  ἐρχόμενον κατὰ πόντον ὑπὸ Ζεφύροιο ἰωῆς:
IL.4.276  on its way over the sea before the drive of the west wind;
IL.4.277  τῷ δέ τ' ἄνευθεν ἐόντι μελάντερον ἠΰτε πίσσα
IL.4.277  far away though he be he watches it, blacker than pitch is,
IL.4.278  φαίνετ' ἰὸν κατὰ πόντον, ἄγει δέ τε λαίλαπα πολλήν,
IL.4.278  moving across the sea and piling the storm before it,
IL.4.279  ῥίγησέν τε ἰδών, ὑπό τε σπέος ἤλασε μῆλα:
IL.4.279  and as he sees it he shivers and drives his flocks to a cavern;
IL.4.280  τοῖαι ἅμ' Αἰάντεσσι διοτρεφέων αἰζηῶν
IL.4.280  so about the two Aiantes moved the battalions,
IL.4.281  δήϊον ἐς πόλεμον πυκιναὶ κίνυντο φάλαγγες
IL.4.281  close-compacted of strong and god-supported young fighters,
IL.4.282  κυάνεαι, σάκεσίν τε καὶ ἔγχεσι πεφρικυῖαι.
IL.4.282  black, and jagged with spear and shield, to the terror of battle.
IL.4.283  καὶ τοὺς μὲν γήθησεν ἰδὼν κρείων Ἀγαμέμνων,
IL.4.283  Agamemnon the lord of men was glad when he looked at them,
IL.4.284  καί σφεας φωνήσας ἔπεα πτερόεντα προσηύδα:

34

IL.4.284   and he spoke aloud to them and addressed them in winged words:

Thus, Agamemnon's emotions, like the goatherd's, are complex, and cannot be reduced to the happiness stated (γήθησεν [283]) in the tenor of the simile. In fact, the goatherd is not happy at all to see the storm-cloud but rather struck with fear (ῥίγησέν [279]), the same verb used to describe Ajax when he fears that Hector's success against him in their duel in Book 16 is the result of divine will and reflects the ability of the gods to bring about whatever results they wish:

IL.16.119   γνῶ δ' Αἴας κατὰ θυμὸν ἀμύμονα ῥίγησέν τε
IL.16.119   And Ajax knew in his blameless heart, and shivered for knowing it, how this
IL.16.120   ἔργα θεῶν, ὅ ῥα πάγχυ μάχης ἐπὶ μήδεα κεῖρε
IL.16.120   was gods' work, how Zeus high-thundering cut across the intention
IL.16.121   Ζεὺς ὑψιβρεμέτης, Τρώεσσι δὲ βούλετο νίκην:
IL.16.121   in all his battle, how he planned that the Trojans should conquer.

Therefore, the salient emotion of the simile in question is anxiety rather than happiness. Yet at the same time it qualifies Agamemnon's happiness, which inspires the simile in the first place. Thus, in this simile Homer employs meta-audience to foreground the spectatorial component of the narrative while avoiding apostrophe or some other equally phatic expedient, which would temporarily shatter the fictional dream. As such, the usefulness of the device is clearly not dependent upon the military subject matter of the *Iliad*.

Vignette, the imaginary equivalent to meta-audience, may also be employed in similes. In Book 4, for example, the color of the wound Menelaos receives from Pandaros' arrow is compared to that of an equestrian object:

IL.4.141   ὡς δ' ὅτε τίς τ' ἐλέφαντα γυνὴ φοίνικι μιήνη
IL.4.141   As when some Maionian woman or Karian with purple
IL.4.142   Μηονὶς ἠὲ Κάειρα παρήϊον ἔμμεναι ἵππων:
IL.4.142   colours ivory, to make it a cheek piece for horses;

After introducing this παρήϊον, Homer transports us even further into the Elsewhere than the simile itself has already brought us,

IL.4.143  κεῖται δ' ἐν θαλάμῳ, πολέες τέ μιν ἠρήσαντο
IL.4.143  it lies away in an inner room, and many a rider
IL.4.144  ἱππῆες φορέειν: βασιλῆϊ δὲ κεῖται ἄγαλμα,
IL.4.144  longs to have it, but it is laid up to be a king's treasure,
IL.4.145  ἀμφότερον κόσμός θ' ἵππῳ ἐλατῆρί τε κῦδος:
IL.4.145  two things, to be the beauty of the horse, the pride of the horseman:

requiring us to inhabit a realm two steps removed from the first-order reality of the primary narrative, on a meta-narrative level one step removed from the fantasy-realm initially visualized in lines 141-42. Homer's transposition of the four devices to the simile-realm of the *Iliad* underscores their centrality to the extradiegetic component of the narrative despite a diegetic context that accommodates them seamlessly and ostensibly inevitably.

Homer uses decomposition, intercutting, meta-audience, and vignette to focus the audience's attention wherever on the dramatic canvas he wishes to, a prerogative he shares with the filmmaker and which distinguishes them both from the playwright. To ascertain this aspect of Homeric artistry, we are concerned with the direct experience of the *Iliad* rather than with data that can be deduced from a paraphrase of this experience. That is, we are concerned with space rather than time. Whereas the execution of each of the devices requires time to unfold, the salient dimension from the standpoint of reception is space, because, as Arnheim puts it:

...it takes things to serve as vehicles for action and...therefore in perception things are prior to what they do. Things, however, dwell in space, whereas time applies to action.[118]

In the *Iliad* we watch characters watch (meta-audience), imagine (vignette), and meet (intercutting) each other, and ourselves, as surrogate characters, penetrate the scene (decomposition), all by means of the "vehicles for action" that are discourse spaces. These four devices serve as the means by which Homer entrenches his audience in the action and

---

[118] 1986: 78.

engages them in a drama whose impact cannot be epitomized, reduced to facts *about* this experience.

According to Samuel Eliot Bassett:

The cinema has at last made possible an epic drama, but must go to Homer before it can fully realize it.[119]

Just as the frame is the primary link between audience and action, so the *kinesis* of frames is the basis for a dedicated approach to narrative space that privileges this fundamental relationship.

---

[119] 1938: 48.

# CHAPTER TWO

# DECOMPOSITION

"Homer…disperses the image of his object over a kind of history of it." (Lessing: 83)

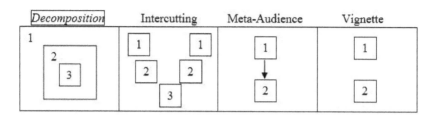

"Decomposition" is the term used by cinema theorists to describe the gradual progression of frames from a more or less distant to a more or less proximate perspective on a given scene.[120] Early filmmakers considered decomposition, and in particular the use of the close-up, to be the most revolutionary aspect of the cinematic art form,[121] transcending the inherent z-axis staticity of theater.[122] It is used, however, quite frequently by Homer, and especially in the *Iliad*.[123] In the *Iliad* Homer rarely gives the audience the impression that they are watching a scene unfold the way it would appear to them on a theater stage. Rather, he transports them into and back out from the action while at the same time preserving their real-world identity as distant spectators. Nick Browne expresses this paradox in cinematic terms:

The filmic image...implies the ambiguity of a double origin—both from my literal place as spectator and from the place where the camera is within the imaginative space.[124]

---

[120] Cf. Feldman (1952: 100).

[121] Cf. Feldman (1952: 98); Arnheim (1957: 76).

[122] Arnheim (1957: 81, 85). That is not to say that theater completely lacks the decompositional impulse. Lutwack (1984: 59), for example, sees it in Shakespeare.

[123] Cf. Edwards (1987: 86); Richardson (1990: 121).

[124] 1999: 161.

Decomposition usually begins with a long shot or extreme long shot and ends with a close-up or extreme close-up, with one or more intermediary shots (such as medium, medium long, or medium close-up) interspersed between them:[125]

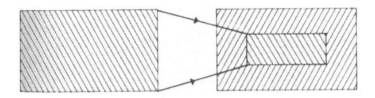

The opposite process, the progression from close-up to long shot, is occasionally used to reveal a scene to the audience gradually rather than instantaneously,[126]

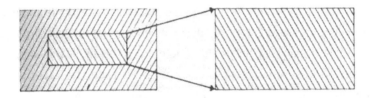

as when the camera pulls back at the beginning of the film "A Clockwork Orange":

The opening memorable image is an intimate closeup of the blue staring eyes and smirking face of ebullient young punker Alex...As the camera zoom pulls back, the anti-hero character with the malevolent, cold stare is shown sitting amidst his kingly court of teenaged gang of "droogs."[127]

---

[125] Cf. Feldman (1958: 101). This capacity of the Homeric audience to function simultaneously as static spectator and dynamic participant is encoded in the very language Homer uses, and in particular in the term δίφρος, which means either "chair" or "chariot," depending upon the context. In their capacity as narrative agents, the audience occupies a δίφρος in the sense of a "chair" or a "chariot" depending upon whether the action is presented to them from long shot or close-up range, respectively.

[126] Cf. Arnheim (1957: 79-80).

[127] Dirks, 1996.

In the scene between Hera and Hephaestus at the end of Book 1 of the *Iliad*, Homer gradually pulls back, like Stanley Kubrick's camera, from a close-up of a small object (κύπελλον [596]) and reveals a meta-audience (τοῖς ἄλλοισι θεοῖς...πᾶσιν [597]) about whose presence we were previously unaware:[128]

IL.1.595 ὣς φάτο, μείδησεν δὲ θεὰ λευκώλενος Ἥρη,
IL.1.595 He spoke, and the goddess of the white arms Hera smiled at him,
IL.1.596 μειδήσασα δὲ παιδὸς ἐδέξατο χειρὶ κύπελλον:
IL.1.596 and smiling she accepted the goblet out of her son's hand.
IL.1.597 αὐτὰρ ὃ τοῖς ἄλλοισι θεοῖς ἐνδέξια πᾶσιν
IL.1.597 Thereafter beginning from the left he poured drinks for the other
IL.1.598 ᾠνοχόει γλυκὺ νέκταρ ἀπὸ κρητῆρος ἀφύσσων:
IL.1.598 gods, dipping up from the mixing bowl the sweet nectar.

Although decomposition entertains frame-change in both directions, from distant to close (approach decomposition) and from close to distant (retreat decomposition),[129] the former is more common in the *Iliad* than the latter. In either case, the fundamental units of this device are the close-up and the long shot.[130] The long shot[131] represents the default distance of the audience from the action, to which they are subsequently granted increased intimacy through medium shots and close-ups. It provides the audience with the view they would have if a scene were to be presented to them in a theater.[132] The most common terms Homer uses to establish long shot range fall under three categories: characters,[133]

---

[128] Along these lines, Edwards (1987: 87) points out the proto-cinematic nature of "the final receding view of Hector's tomb (24.804)."

[129] Cf. Feldman (1952: 100).

[130] Cf. Arnheim (1957: 79).

[131] Cf. Feldman (1952: 182).

[132] Since we are speaking of the "theater of the mind," however, the Homeric audience's perspective on the action encompasses a much greater amount of territory than a physical theater can, accommodating, for example, such spectacles as "...the long shot of the burning pyres that represent the results of Apollo's plague (1.52)..." (Edwards, 1987: 87); cf. Lowe (2000: 42).

[133] army (στρατός)

    *Il*. 4.436 ὣς Τρώων ἀλαλητὸς ἀνὰ στρατὸν εὐρὺν ὀρώρει:

    *Il*. 4.436 the crying of the Trojans went up through the wide army.

landmarks,[134] and implements.[135] The close-up[136] brings the audience

---

assembly (ἀγορὴ)

*Il.* 7.345   Τρώων δ' αὖτ' ἀγορὴ γένετ' Ἰλίου ἐν πόλει ἄκρῃ

*Il.* 7.345   Now there was an assembly of Trojans high on the city of Ilion

people (λαός)

*Il.* 7.306   τὼ δὲ διακρινθέντε ὃ μὲν μετὰ λαὸν Ἀχαιῶν

*Il.* 7.306   So separating, Aias went among the Achaian people,

throng (ὅμιλος)

*Il.* 11.246   δὴ τότε γ' Ἀτρεΐδης Ἀγαμέμνων ἐξενάριξε,

*Il.* 11.246   Now Agamemnon, son of Atreus, stripped him and went back

*Il.* 11.247   βῆ δὲ φέρων ἀν' ὅμιλον Ἀχαιῶν τεύχεα καλά.

*Il.* 11.247   to the throng of the Achaians bearing the splendid armour.

[134] plain (πεδίον)

*Il.* 6.2   πολλὰ δ' ἄρ' ἔνθα καὶ ἔνθ' ἴθυσε μάχη πεδίοιο

*Il.* 6.2   and the battle veered greatly now one way, now in another,

sky (οὐρανός)

*Il.* 19.257   εὐξάμενος δ' ἄρα εἶπεν ἰδὼν εἰς οὐρανὸν εὐρύν:

*Il.* 19.257   He spoke before them in prayer gazing into the wide sky:

sea (πόντος, θάλασσα), shore (θίς):

*Il.* 1.34   βῆ δ' ἀκέων παρὰ θῖνα πολυφλοίσβοιο θαλάσσης:

*Il.* 1.34   and went silently away beside the murmuring sea beach.

river (ποταμὸς)

*Il.* 21.303   ...οὐδέ μιν ἔσχεν

*Il.* 21.303   ...the river wide running

*Il.* 21.304   εὐρὺ ῥέων ποταμός...

*Il.* 21.304   could not stop him now...

shelter (κλισία)

*Il.* 2.399   κάπνισσάν τε κατὰ κλισίας, καὶ δεῖπνον ἕλοντο.

*Il.* 2.399   they kindled the fires' smoke along the shelters, and took their dinner,

[135] ship (ναῦς)

*Il.* 10.136   βῆ δ' ἰέναι κατὰ νῆας Ἀχαιῶν χαλκοχιτώνων.

*Il.* 10.136   and went on his way down the ships of the bronze-armoured Achaians.

horse (ἵππος)

*Il.* 4.365   εὗρε δὲ Τυδέος υἱὸν ὑπέρθυμον Διομήδεα

*Il.* 4.365   He came on the son of Tydeus, high-spirited Diomedes,

*Il.* 4.366   ἑσταότ' ἔν θ' ἵπποισι καὶ ἅρμασι κολλητοῖσι:

*Il.* 4.366   standing among the compacted chariots and by the horses,

fire (πῦρ)

*Il.* 8.553   οἳ δὲ μέγα φρονέοντες ἐπὶ πτολέμοιο γεφύρῃ

*Il.* 8.553   So with hearts made high these sat night-long by the outworks

within touching range of a character or object, providing firsthand access to, rather than merely spectatorial distance from,[137] the action, functioning either to intensify[138] or to generate suspense within[139] a given scene.[140] The most common close-up terms fall under two categories: body-parts[141] and implements.[142]

---

*Il.* 8.554   εἴατο παννύχιοι, πυρὰ δέ σφισι καίετο πολλά.

*Il.* 8.554   of battle, and their watchfires blazed numerous about them.

[136] Cf. Feldman (1952: 182).

[137] Cf. Goffman (1974: 144); Arnheim (1957: 85); Münsterberg (1970: 38).

[138] Cf. Pudovkin (1960: 90).

[139] Cf. Chatman (1981b: 124-25).

[140] For Münsterberg (1970: 37) the close-up represents the most unique aspect of cinematic artistry.

[141] eye (ὄσσε)

*Il.* 1.199   θάμβησεν δ' Ἀχιλεύς, μετὰ δ' ἐτράπετ', αὐτίκα δ' ἔγνω

*Il.* 1.199   Achilleus in amazement turned about, and straightway

*Il.* 1.200   Παλλάδ' Ἀθηναίην: δεινὼ δέ οἱ ὄσσε φάανθεν:

*Il.* 1.200   knew Pallas Athena and the terrible eyes shining.

head (κεφαλή)

*Il.* 24.682 στῆ δ' ἄρ' ὑπὲρ κεφαλῆς καί μιν πρὸς μῦθον ἔειπεν:

*Il.* 24.682 He stood above his head and spoke a word to him, saying:

hand (χείρ)

*Il.* 14.232   ἔν τ' ἄρα οἱ φῦ χειρὶ ἔπος τ' ἔφατ' ἔκ τ' ὀνόμαζεν:

*Il.* 14.232   She clung fast to his hand and spoke a word and called him by name: 'Sleep,

tear (δάκρυον)

*Il.* 6.459   καί ποτέ τις εἴπησιν ἰδὼν κατὰ δάκρυ χέουσαν:

*Il.* 6.459   and some day seeing you shedding a tear a man will say of you:

[142] sword (ξίφος)

*Il.* 3.361   Ἀτρεΐδης δὲ ἐρυσσάμενος ξίφος ἀργυρόηλον

*Il.* 3.361   Drawing his sword with the silver nails, the son of Atreus

spear (δόρυ, ἔγχος)

*Il.* 4.490   Πριαμίδης καθ' ὅμιλον ἀκόντισεν ὀξέϊ δουρί.

*Il.* 4.490   Priam's son, made a cast at him in the crowd with the sharp spear

bow (βιός)

*Il.* 1.49   δεινὴ δὲ κλαγγὴ γένετ' ἀργυρέοιο βιοῖο:

*Il.* 1.49   Terrible was the clash that rose from the bow of silver.

helmet (κόρυς)

*Il.* 3.369   ἦ καὶ ἐπαΐξας κόρυθος λάβεν ἱπποδασείης,

Because the verbal equivalent of a long shot, medium shot, or close-up view of a character or object is achieved through words rather than pictures, there are theoretically as many potential distances between audience and action as there are characters or objects to refer to. Therefore, to avoid spatial ambiguity and to increase the degree of control he exerts over his audience's attention, Homer limits the number of terms he uses with any degree of regularity to represent long shot and close-up distances,[143] thereby compensating for the inherent semantic fluidity of the verbal sign.[144] This endows the privileged terms that survive this process with a pseudo-iconic quality that, according to cinematographer Edward Dmytryk, is exclusive to cinema:

A semantic axiom states that *words* are signs for *things*, but only in a generic sense. To make things more specific words must be modified by *other* words, and it often requires a paragraph of modifiers to pin a word down to a sign of a *particular* thing. *Shots*, on the other hand, are by their nature already signs for particular things—a shot of an airliner, for instance, will identify it specifically as, say, an American Airlines 747 rather than just an "airplane"—and are therefore much more real than words, semantically speaking.[145]

By reducing the shot repertoire at his disposal to a small number of items representing long shot and close-up distances, however, Homer constructs a spatial vocabulary whose terms attain the "real" quality Dmytryk attributes to pictures.[146] Each spatial *sema*[147] possesses a kind of iconic quality: by directing our eye to the same specific region of the

---

*Il.* 3.369   He spoke, and flashing forward laid hold of the horse-haired helmet

[143] The medium shot ("A medium shot neither magnifies nor reduces the size of what is seen upon the screen…the medium shot…regarded as the norm." [Feldman, 1952: 182]) is more ambiguous than either the long shot or the close-up, occupying the intermediary region between them, spanning the range from medium close-up to medium long shot. As such, the medium shot resists codification and is most often represented simply by naming a character either out of the blue or within a decompositional series.

[144] Cf. Culler (1986: 50).

[145] 1988: 87.

[146] Cf. Eades/Létoublon (1999: 312); Lutwack (1984: 17); Fischer-Lichte (1992: 110); Osadnik (1994: 213); Pudovkin (1960: 23).

[147] Cf. Foley (1999, 13-14).

narrative canvas each time it is mentioned, it attains a power over our perceptive machinery analogous to that of the cinematic image. Like a close-up of a hand that fills the screen, certain Homeric *semata* focus our attention no less unambiguously upon a particular object than a photographic enlargement does. This enables Homer to exert proportionately greater control over his narrative canvas through the immediacy of *enargeia*.

Homer achieves shot variety in several ways, exploiting the scenographic precision that his spatial code makes available to him. Indeed, the use of close-ups and long shots is not limited to decomposition. Therefore, before we turn to decomposition proper we should consider how Homer uses these shots in combinations other than decompositionally *per se*.[148] Sometimes he cuts immediately from long shot to close-up, without the use of medium shots to mitigate the transition.[149] At the beginning of Book 1, for example, when Chryses travels to the Greek camp to ransom his daughter Chryseis, the frame shifts between ἐπὶ νῆας (12) and ἐν χερσὶν (14), two of the most frequently used phrases to express long shot and close-up distances, respectively:

IL.1.12   Ἀτρεΐδης· ὃ γὰρ ἦλθε θοὰς ἐπὶ νῆας Ἀχαιῶν
IL.1.12   when he came beside the fast ships of the Achaians to ransom
IL.1.13   λυσόμενός τε θύγατρα φέρων τ' ἀπερείσι' ἄποινα,
IL.1.13   back his daughter, carrying gifts beyond count and holding
IL.1.14   στέμματ' ἔχων ἐν χερσὶν ἑκηβόλου Ἀπόλλωνος
IL.1.14   in his hands wound on a staff of gold the ribbons of Apollo
IL.1.15   χρυσέῳ ἀνὰ σκήπτρῳ, καὶ ἐλίσσετο πάντας Ἀχαιούς,
IL.1.15   who strikes from afar, and supplicated all the Achaians,
IL.1.16   Ἀτρεΐδα δὲ μάλιστα δύω, κοσμήτορε λαῶν·

---

[148] The alternation between close-ups and long shots to vary the presentation of the action and to avoid monotony is a central preoccupation of cinema (cf. Arnheim [1957: 81)]). As Joseph Feldman (1952: 204) points out: "It is as important to create the rhythm of a movement or an action in a film by modulating the cutting beat as it is to represent it visually and pictorially. A photograph of a movement or an action in a film is a dead thing until it has been rendered alive by rhythm. Cf. also Pudovkin (1960: 131).
[149] Cf. Arnheim (1957: 83).

IL.1.16  but above all Atreus' two sons, the marshals of the people:

Homer may also cut from long shot to medium shot, foregoing close-up range altogether. This is most effective when the dramatic focus is on extensive dialogue, when the conceptual dimension of the narrative is emphasized:

IL.1.57  οἳ δ' ἐπεὶ οὖν ἤγερθεν ὁμηγερέες τ' ἐγένοντο,
IL.1.57  Now when they were all assembled in one place together,
IL.1.58  τοῖσι δ' ἀνιστάμενος μετέφη πόδας ὠκὺς Ἀχιλλεύς:
IL.1.58  Achilles of the swift feet stood up among them and spoke forth:

A shot from one range, however, does not always gravitate toward another. Homer frequently combines long shots or close-ups in clusters, to maintain a consistent distance between audience and action. In the following scene we travel to several different locations in a series of long shots linked seamlessly rather than interrupted abruptly by close-ups or medium shots, fostering a contemplative survey of the distant action and, in lines 488-89, putting the otherwise larger-than-life Achilles into proper scenographic (and cosmic) perspective:[150]

IL.1.477  ἦμος δ' ἠριγένεια φάνη ῥοδοδάκτυλος Ἠώς,
IL.1.477  But when the young Dawn showed again with her rosy fingers,
IL.1.478  καὶ τότ' ἔπειτ' ἀνάγοντο μετὰ στρατὸν εὐρὺν Ἀχαιῶν:
IL.1.478  they put forth to sea toward the wide camp of the Achaians.
IL.1.483  ἣ δ' ἔθεεν κατὰ κῦμα διαπρήσσουσα κέλευθον.
IL.1.483  She ran swiftly cutting across the swell her pathway.
IL.1.484  αὐτὰρ ἐπεί ῥ' ἵκοντο μετὰ στρατὸν εὐρὺν Ἀχαιῶν,
IL.1.484  But when they had come back to the wide camp of the Achaians
IL.1.485  νῆα μὲν οἵ γε μέλαιναν ἐπ' ἠπείροιο ἔρυσσαν
IL.1.485  they hauled the black ship up on the mainland, high up
IL.1.486  ὑψοῦ ἐπὶ ψαμάθοις, ὑπὸ δ' ἕρματα μακρὰ τάνυσσαν:
IL.1.486  on the sand, and underneath her they fixed the long props.
IL.1.487  αὐτοὶ δ' ἐσκίδναντο κατὰ κλισίας τε νέας τε.
IL.1.487  Afterwards they scattered to their own ships and their shelters.
IL.1.488  αὐτὰρ ὃ μήνιε νηυσὶ παρήμενος ὠκυπόροισι
IL.1.488  But that other still sat in anger beside his swift ships,
IL.1.489  διογενὴς Πηλέως υἱὸς πόδας ὠκὺς Ἀχιλλεύς:

---

[150] Stern (1979:67) attributes this technique to Griffith.

IL.1.489   Peleus' son divinely born, Achilles of the swift feet.

This long shot cluster prepares us for Thetis' ascent to Olympus in the following lines and a decompositional series culminating in a close-up of her hand touching Zeus' chin as she supplicates him to grant Achilles' request to punish the Greeks for Agamemnon's affront to his honor. The consistent use of long shots in the previous scene increases the already substantial impact produced by the contrast between long shot and close-up in the decompositional series itself.

Close-ups can also be combined over two or more shots to emphasize the intimacy achieved between the characters in question. When Aphrodite returns to Olympus after being wounded by Diomedes in Book 5, for example, the close-up cluster preceding Dione's words adds pathos to the scene by drawing the audience into the exclusive emotional sphere of mother and daughter:

IL.5.370   ἣ δ' ἐν γούνασι πῖπτε Διώνης δῖ' Ἀφροδίτη
IL.5.370   and now bright Aphrodite fell at the knees of her mother,
IL.5.371   μητρὸς ἑῆς: ἣ δ' ἀγκὰς ἐλάζετο θυγατέρα ἥν,
IL.5.371   Dione, who gathered her daughter into the arms' fold
IL.5.372   χειρί τέ μιν κατέρεξεν ἔπος τ' ἔφατ' ἔκ τ' ὀνόμαζε:
IL.5.372   and stroked her with her hand and called her by name and spoke to her:

When Achilles prays to his mother in Book 1, the continuity of close-up range between lines 357 and 361 is preserved despite the intermediary transition to Thetis' maritime abode, emphasizing the transcendent bond between the two characters, impervious to mere physical distance:

IL.1.357   ὣς φάτο δάκρυ χέων, τοῦ δ' ἔκλυε πότνια μήτηρ
IL.1.357   So he spoke in tears and the lady his mother heard him
IL.1.358   ἡμένη ἐν βένθεσσιν ἁλὸς παρὰ πατρὶ γέροντι:
IL.1.358   as she sat in the depths of the sea at the side of her aged father,
IL.1.359   καρπαλίμως δ' ἀνέδυ πολιῆς ἁλὸς ἠΰτ' ὀμίχλη,
IL.1.359   and lightly she emerged like a mist from the grey water.
IL.1.360   καί ῥα πάροιθ' αὐτοῖο καθέζετο δάκρυ χέοντος,
IL.1.360   She came and sat beside him as he wept, and stroked him
IL.1.361   χειρί τέ μιν κατέρεξεν ἔπος τ' ἔφατ' ἔκ τ' ὀνόμαζε:
IL.1.361   with her hand and called him by name and spoke to him:

Although Homer employs an extensive repertoire of long shots and close-ups to vary his presentation, he is nevertheless best able to exploit the full range of z-axis artistry by including intermediary shots between these two extreme distances. It is thus to decomposition proper that we now turn.

Decomposition is more common in the *Iliad* than in the *Odyssey*, corresponding to their montagistic and realistic orientations, respectively. While the *Iliad* promotes z-axis penetration, the *Odyssey* consistently keeps the audience at bay, providing two- rather than three-dimensional access to the action. Therefore, Odyssean close-ups usually play a functional rather than stylistic role, serving more to accentuate the emotional content of a given scene than to transport the audience into the action. Thus, when Homer uses close-ups in the *Odyssey*, he frequently dampens their impact by qualifying them with abstract adjectives that impart to them a melodramatic quality. When he uses the term "tears," for example, he often accompanies it with adverbial, adjectival, and verbal emotional cues such as στοναχῇσι καὶ ἄλγεσι (5.83), ἐλεεινὸν (8.531), and ὀδύρετο (16.214), respectively, resulting in a receptive detachment from the image in question that privileges its conceptual rather than its perceptual dimension, a tendency that Peisistratos makes overt in his encomium to tears in Book 4, which induces us to take his use of δάκρυ in line 198, following ὀδυρόμενος (192) and κλαίειν (196), figuratively rather than literally:

OD.4.193  καὶ νῦν, εἴ τί που ἔστι, πίθοιό μοι: οὐ γὰρ ἔγωγε
OD.4.193  So now, if it may be, would you do me a favor? For my part
OD.4.194  τέρπομ' ὀδυρόμενος μεταδόρπιος, ἀλλὰ καὶ ἠὼς
OD.4.194  I have no joy in tears after dinnertime. There will always
OD.4.195  ἔσσεται ἠριγένεια: νεμεσσῶμαί γε μὲν οὐδὲν
OD.4.195  be a new dawn tomorrow. Yet I can have no objection
OD.4.196  κλαίειν ὅς κε θάνῃσι βροτῶν καὶ πότμον ἐπίσπῃ.
OD.4.196  to tears for any mortal who dies and goes to his destiny.
OD.4.197  τοῦτό νυ καὶ γέρας οἶον ὀιζυροῖσι βροτοῖσι,
OD.4.197  And this is the only consolation we wretched mortals
OD.4.198  κείρασθαί τε κόμην βαλέειν τ' ἀπὸ δάκρυ παρειῶν.
OD.4.198  can give, to cut our hair and let the tears roll down our faces.

That is not to say, however, that the *Odyssey* does not occasionally exploit z-axis *kinesis* as well, as in the following use of retreat decomposition, which achieves a similar effect as the Hephaestus passage quoted above:

OD.7.142   ἀμφὶ δ' ἄρ' Ἀρήτης βάλε γούνασι χεῖρας Ὀδυσσεύς,
OD.7.142   Odysseus clasped Arete's knees in his arms, and at that time
OD.7.143   καὶ τότε δή ῥ' αὐτοῖο πάλιν χύτο θέσφατος ἀήρ.
OD.7.143   the magical and surrounding mist was drifted from him,
OD.7.144   οἱ δ' ἄνεω ἐγένοντο, δόμον κάτα φῶτα ἰδόντες:
OD.7.144   and all fell silent through the house when they saw the man there,
OD.7.145   θαύμαζον δ' ὁρόωντες. ὁ δ' ἐλλιτάνευεν Ὀδυσσεύς:
OD.7.145   and they wondered looking on him, and Odysseus made his entreaty:

In such cases, however, the transition from one range to another is abrupt, unrelieved by intermediary distances, presenting the scene as economically as possible. When Menelaos encounters Telemachus in Book 4, for example, the process is abbreviated, like a cinematic jump cut:[151]

OD.4.310   βῆ δ' ἴμεν ἐκ θαλάμοιο θεῷ ἐναλίγκιος ἄντην,
OD.4.310   He went on his way from the chamber, like a god in presence,
OD.4.311   Τηλεμάχῳ δὲ παρῖζεν, ἔπος τ' ἔφατ' ἔκ τ' ὀνόμαζε:
OD.4.311   and sat down by Telemachos and spoke to him and named him:

While decomposition is a z-axis phenomenon, enabling the audience to penetrate the action, the *Odyssey* compensates for its predominant two-dimensionality by employing a kind of x-axis substitute for its Iliadic counterpart. In this case, however, the audience is invited into the action, not directly as with decomposition proper, but rather indirectly, through a character's own meta-z-axis perspective. This diegetic variety of decomposition corresponds to the *Odyssey*'s horizontal orientation, according to which interiors are constantly penetrated by characters within the story. It reveals itself most conspicuously in the five ecphrases of the *Odyssey*, all of which describe the penetration of an enclosure,

---

[151] Cf. Phillips (1999: 572).

49

whether a cave (Calypso's [5.63-74]), a palace (Antinoos' [7.81-132]), or a harbor (Goat Island [9.116-41], Land of the Laistrygones [10.87-99], Ithaca [13.96-112]). In each case the decompositional process culminates in Odysseus either walking or sailing into a given interior. Thus, Homer adapts this originally montagistic device to a realistic context, linking discrete spaces through panning[152] rather than cutting, thereby distinguishing itself from Iliadic decomposition.

The most common decompositional series in the *Iliad* is the transition from long shot to medium shot to close-up, in which a character moves progressively closer to another character and ultimately engages him or her in conversation. Often an immortal descends from Olympus and locates, approaches, and addresses a mortal within medium or close-up range, as in Book 2 when Dream obeys Zeus' request to visit Agamemnon and to persuade him to urge his troops to leave Troy:

IL.2.16  ὣς φάτο, βῆ δ' ἄρ' ὄνειρος ἐπεὶ τὸν μῦθον ἄκουσε:
IL.2.16  So he spoke, and Dream listened to his word and descended.
IL.2.17  καρπαλίμως δ' ἵκανε θοὰς ἐπὶ νῆας Ἀχαιῶν,
IL.2.17  Lightly he came down beside the swift ships of the Achaians
IL.2.18  βῆ δ' ἄρ' ἐπ' Ἀτρεΐδην Ἀγαμέμνονα: τὸν δ' ἐκίχανεν
IL.2.18  and came to Agamemnon the son of Atreus. He found him
IL.2.19  εὕδοντ' ἐν κλισίῃ, περὶ δ' ἀμβρόσιος κέχυθ' ὕπνος.
IL.2.19  sleeping within his shelter in a cloud of immortal slumber.
IL.2.20  στῆ δ' ἄρ' ὑπὲρ κεφαλῆς Νηληΐῳ υἷι ἐοικώς
IL.2.20  Dream stood then beside his head in the likeness of Nestor,

This process can also be reversed, however, as when Ares ascends to Olympus to seek Zeus' support after being wounded by Diomedes on the Trojan plain:[153]

---

[152] Cf. Chatman (1978: 101-02).

[153] In lines 5.793-99, Athena locates Diomedes and initiates a decompositional series that likewise concludes with an extreme close-up of a wound. In the present case, however, Athena begins her search, not from Olympus but having already descended to the Trojan plain with Hera in line 769. The significance of the fact that this construction constitutes a reverse-image of the Ares scene in every detail except the provenience of the deity provides an interesting adumbration of Odyssean protocol, when Athena's earth-bound status becomes the rule rather than the exception.

IL.5.864 οἵη δ' ἐκ νεφέων ἐρεβεννὴ φαίνεται ἀὴρ
IL.5.864 As when out of the thunderhead the air shows darkening
IL.5.865 καύματος ἐξ ἀνέμοιο δυσαέος ὀρνυμένοιο,
IL.5.865 after a day's heat when the stormy wind uprises,
IL.5.866 τοῖος Τυδεΐδῃ Διομήδεϊ χάλκεος Ἄρης
IL.5.866 thus to Tydeus' son Diomedes Ares the brazen
IL.5.867 φαίνεθ' ὁμοῦ νεφέεσσιν ἰὼν εἰς οὐρανὸν εὐρύν.
IL.5.867 showed as he went up with the clouds into the wide heaven.
IL.5.868 καρπαλίμως δ' ἵκανε θεῶν ἕδος αἰπὺν Ὄλυμπον,
IL.5.868 Lightly he came to the gods' citadel, headlong Olympos,
IL.5.869 πὰρ δὲ Διὶ Κρονίωνι καθέζετο θυμὸν ἀχεύων,
IL.5.869 and sat down beside Kronian Zeus, grieving in his spirit,
IL.5.870 δεῖξεν δ' ἄμβροτον αἷμα καταρρέον ἐξ ὠτειλῆς,
IL.5.870 and showed him the immortal blood dripping from the spear cut.

Because the decompositional process represents a fundamental relationship between the audience and the action that transcends any particular subject matter it might deal with, the device occasionally manifests itself on the microstructural level as well. In Book 16, for example, Homer underscores Achilles' rare appearance within his shelter by presenting his actions there decompositionally, although involving uncustomary items for this purpose. First the audience penetrates Achilles' shelter,

IL.16.220 ...αὐτὰρ Ἀχιλλεὺς
IL.16.220 ...But meanwhile Achilleus
IL.16.221 βῆ ῥ' ἴμεν ἐς κλισίην, χηλοῦ δ' ἀπὸ πῶμ' ἀνέῳγε...
IL.16.221 went off into his shelter, and lifted the lid from a lovely chest...

then the chest within his shelter,

IL.16.225 ἔνθα δέ οἱ δέπας ἔσκε τετυγμένον...
IL.16.225 Inside this lay a wrought goblet...

IL.16.228 τό ῥα τότ' ἐκ χηλοῖο λαβὼν...
IL.16.228 Taking this now out of the chest...

and finally the goblet within the chest:

IL.16.230 ...|ἀφύσσατο δ' αἴθοπα οἶνον|.
IL.16.230 ...he poured shining wine [into the goblet].

While most decompositional series involve the gradual unfolding of a single action, the momentum from long shot to close-up is so strong that it occasionally violates this principle and extends from a long shot of one subject to a close-up of another subject. This phenomenon occurs in cinema as well. In the Tom Tykwer movie "Heaven," for example, the protagonist Philippa walks briskly down a long corridor, followed by an extremely slow tracking shot. By the time she reaches the end of the corridor and turns left, the camera remains far behind, much closer to where it began than to the end of the corridor. Once she takes the turn, we cut to the interior of a public restroom, facing a door through which she enters immediately. As she approaches us the camera continues creeping along toward her at apparently the same speed as it was moving along the corridor. Thus, although the scene has changed from the corridor to the bathroom, the camera movement remains the same, as though operating autonomously, according to its own transcendent agenda. This variety of decomposition also occurs in the *Iliad*, when a series begins in one milieu but then at some point switches to another without breaking sequence. For example, in the lines leading up to the Aphrodite/Dione encounter mentioned above, the scene shifts from a long shot of Iris ascending to Olympus and feeding her horses, to a medium shot of Aphrodite and Dione, and finally to a close-up of Dione's hand:

IL.5.367 αἶψα δ' ἔπειθ' ἵκοντο θεῶν ἕδος αἰπὺν Ὄλυμπον:
IL.5.367 Now as they came to sheer Olympos, the place of the immortals,
IL.5.368 ἔνθ' ἵππους ἔστησε ποδήνεμος ὠκέα Ἶρις
IL.5.368 there swift Iris the wind-footed reined in her horses
IL.5.369 λύσασ' ἐξ ὀχέων, παρὰ δ' ἀμβρόσιον βάλεν εἶδαρ:
IL.5.369 and slipped them from the yoke and threw fodder immortal before them,
IL.5.370 ἣ δ' ἐν γούνασι πῖπτε Διώνης δῖ' Ἀφροδίτη
IL.5.370 and now bright Aphrodite fell at the knees of her mother,
IL.5.371 μητρὸς ἑῆς: ἣ δ' ἀγκὰς ἐλάζετο θυγατέρα ἥν,
IL.5.371 Dione, who gathered her daughter into the arms' fold
IL.5.372 χειρί τέ μιν κατέρεξεν ἔπος τ' ἔφατ' ἐκ τ' ὀνόμαζε:

IL.5.372　and stroked her with her hand and called her by name and spoke to her:

The transition between lines 369 and 370 sustains the decompositional process despite a change in subjects. This also occurs at the end of Book 24, when Priam returns to Troy with Hector's corpse and Homer cuts from a long shot of the singers and women, to a medium shot of the grieving Andromache, and to a close-up of Hector's head:

IL.24.718　ὣς ἔφαθ', οἳ δὲ διέστησαν καὶ εἶξαν ἀπήνῃ.
IL.24.718　So he spoke, and they stood apart and made way for the wagon.
IL.24.719　οἳ δ' ἐπεὶ εἰσάγαγον κλυτὰ δώματα, τὸν μὲν ἔπειτα
IL.24.719　And when they had brought him inside the renowned house, they laid him
IL.24.720　τρητοῖς ἐν λεχέεσσι θέσαν, παρὰ δ' εἷσαν ἀοιδοὺς
IL.24.720　then on a carved bed, and seated beside him the singers
IL.24.721　θρήνων ἐξάρχους, οἵ τε στονόεσσαν ἀοιδὴν
IL.24.721　who were to lead the melody in the dirge, and the singers
IL.24.722　οἳ μὲν ἄρ' ἐθρήνεον, ἐπὶ δὲ στενάχοντο γυναῖκες.
IL.24.722　chanted the song of sorrow, and the women were mourning beside them.
IL.24.723　τῇσιν δ' Ἀνδρομάχη λευκώλενος ἦρχε γόοιο
IL.24.723　Andromache of the white arms led the lamentation
IL.24.724　Ἕκτορος ἀνδροφόνοιο κάρη μετὰ χερσὶν ἔχουσα:
IL.24.724　of the women, and held in her arms the head of manslaughtering Hector:[154]

A decompositional series is often followed by one character (usually the one who finds the other) addressing another character (usually the one who is found), after which one of four scenarios is possible. In the most typical construction, the addressee heeds the speaker's advice and simply initiates the behavior advocated by his or her words, as when Athena urges Odysseus to prevent the Achaeans from taking to heart Agamemnon's recommendation to abandon the war and return to Greece:

IL.2.166　ὣς ἔφατ', οὐδ' ἀπίθησε θεὰ γλαυκῶπις Ἀθήνη,
IL.2.166　So she spoke, nor did the goddess grey-eyed Athene
IL.2.167　βῆ δὲ κατ' Οὐλύμποιο καρήνων ἀΐξασα:
IL.2.167　disobey her, but went in speed down the peaks of Olympos,

---

[154] The impact of this final image is increased by the evocation of Hector's corpse earlier in Book 24 by Priam (406-09, 553-54) and Hermes (411-21) by means of a device called vignette, which is treated in Chapter 6.

IL.2.168    καρπαλίμως δ' ἵκανε θοὰς ἐπὶ νῆας Ἀχαιῶν.

IL.2.168    and lightly she arrived beside the fast ships of the Achaians.

IL.2.169    εὗρεν ἔπειτ' Ὀδυσῆα Διὶ μῆτιν ἀτάλαντον

IL.2.169    There she came on Odysseus, the equal of Zeus in counsel,

IL.2.170    ἑσταότ': οὐδ' ὅ γε νηὸς ἐϋσσέλμοιο μελαίνης

IL.2.170    standing still; he had laid no hand upon his black, strong-benched

IL.2.171    ἅπτετ', ἐπεί μιν ἄχος κραδίην καὶ θυμὸν ἵκανεν:

IL.2.171    vessel, since disappointment touched his heart and his spirit.

IL.2.172    ἀγχοῦ δ' ἱσταμένη προσέφη γλαυκῶπις Ἀθήνη:

IL.2.172    Athene of the grey eyes stood beside him and spoke to him:

IL.2.182    ὣς φάθ', ὃ δὲ ξυνέηκε θεᾶς ὄπα φωνησάσης,

IL.2.182    So she spoke, and he knew the voice of the goddess speaking

IL.2.183    βῆ δὲ θέειν, ἀπὸ δὲ χλαῖναν βάλε: τὴν δ' ἐκόμισσε

IL.2.183    and went on the run, throwing aside his cloak, which was caught up

IL.2.184    κῆρυξ Εὐρυβάτης Ἰθακήσιος ὅς οἱ ὀπήδει:

IL.2.184    by Eurybates the herald of Ithaka who followed him.

In another construction, the addressee responds, after a single line of preliminary description, to the initial speaker, as when Aeneas urges Pandaros to staunch the momentum of Diomedes' *aristeia* in Book 5, initiating a lengthy exchange between the two warriors, over the course of which they agree to team up against the Greek hero:

IL.5.166    τὸν δ' ἴδεν Αἰνείας ἀλαπάζοντα στίχας ἀνδρῶν,

IL.5.166    Now as Aineias saw him wrecking the ranks of warriors

IL.5.167    βῆ δ' ἴμεν ἄν τε μάχην καὶ ἀνὰ κλόνον ἐγχειάων

IL.5.167    he went on his way through the fighting and the spears' confusion

IL.5.168    Πάνδαρον ἀντίθεον διζήμενος εἴ που ἐφεύροι:

IL.5.168    looking to see if he could find Pandaros the godlike;

IL.5.169    εὗρε Λυκάονος υἱὸν ἀμύμονά τε κρατερόν τε,

IL.5.169    and he came upon the strong and blameless son of Lykaon.

IL.5.170    στῆ δὲ πρόσθ' αὐτοῖο ἔπος τέ μιν ἀντίον ηὔδα:

IL.5.170    He stood before him face to face and spoke a word to him:

In a third decompositional construction, the initial speech is followed by several lines of intermediary description, eventually resulting in the addressee delivering a speech of his or her own. During these intervening lines, however, the audience is unsure whether the decompositional series has already run its course, as is usually the case, or will be extended further, resulting in a degree of suspense about the outcome of the scene that manifests itself exclusively through spatial means. When, at the beginning of Book 19, Thetis delivers to Achilles the shield Hephaestus has just made for him, the four-stage progression of the action imparts to the scene an emphatic sense of pseudo-closure:

IL.19.3 ἣ δ' ἐς νῆας ἵκανε θεοῦ πάρα δῶρα φέρουσα.
IL.19.3 And Thetis came to the ships and carried with her the gifts of Hephaestus.
IL.19.4 εὗρε δὲ Πατρόκλῳ περικείμενον ὃν φίλον υἱὸν
IL.19.4 She found her beloved son lying in the arms of Patroclus
IL.19.5 κλαίοντα λιγέως· πολέες δ' ἀμφ' αὐτὸν ἑταῖροι
IL.19.5 crying shrill, and his companions in their numbers about him
IL.19.6 μύρονθ'· ἣ δ' ἐν τοῖσι παρίστατο δῖα θεάων,
IL.19.6 mourned. She, shining among divinities, stood there beside them.
IL.19.7 ἔν τ' ἄρα οἱ φῦ χειρὶ ἔπος τ' ἔφατ' ἔκ τ' ὀνόμαζε·
IL.19.7 She clung to her son's hand and called him by name and spoke to him:

After Thetis speaks, Achilles' reaction to the appearance of his new armor is preceded by four intervening statements, the first two of which distance us from the action via long shot. Because Achilles does not immediately reply to Thetis' words, the construction seems to have exhausted its spatial potential, ripe for transition to a new scene:

IL.19.12 ὡς ἄρα φωνήσασα θεὰ κατὰ τεύχε' ἔθηκε
IL.19.12 The goddess spoke so, and set down the armour on the ground
IL.19.13 πρόσθεν Ἀχιλλῆος· τὰ δ' ἀνέβραχε δαίδαλα πάντα.
IL.19.13 before Achilles, and all its elaboration clashed loudly.
IL.19.14 Μυρμιδόνας δ' ἄρα πάντας ἕλε τρόμος, οὐδέ τις ἔτλη
IL.19.14 Trembling took hold of all the Myrmidons. None had the courage
IL.19.15 ἄντην εἰσιδέειν, ἀλλ' ἔτρεσαν. αὐτὰρ Ἀχιλλεὺς
IL.19.15 to look straight at it. They were afraid of it. Only Achilles

In lines 16-17, Homer imputes to Achilles a response to the armor that, encouraged by that of the Myrmidons in line 14, we might have been tempted to extrapolate for ourselves, with different results, to give closure to the scene. The final position αὐτὰρ Ἀχιλλεὺς in line 15, however, prevents us from taking such liberties. We are rewarded for our patience with a striking close-up of Achilles' eyes in line 17:

IL.19.16 ὡς εἶδ', ὥς μιν μᾶλλον ἔδυ χόλος, ἐν δέ οἱ ὄσσε

55

IL.19.16   looked, and as he looked the anger came harder upon him

IL.19.17   δεινὸν ὑπὸ βλεφάρων ὡς εἰ σέλας ἐξεφάανθεν:

IL.19.17   and his eyes glittered terribly under his lids, like sunflare.

This conveys his anger more forcefully than if we had ourselves interfered, preparing us for the final close-up in line 18 that establishes the intimacy between Achilles and Thetis required for the ensuing dialogue to realize its full dramatic potential:

IL.19.18   τέρπετο δ' ἐν χείρεσσιν ἔχων θεοῦ ἀγλαὰ δῶρα.

IL.19.18   He was glad, holding in his hands the shining gifts of Hephaestus.

The initial-position τέρπετο in line 18 initiates a dramatic shift of emotion from anger to joy, and the close-up of Achilles' hands recalls Thetis' gesture in line 7, tying them together via ring composition and endowing the remaining conversation between mother and son with an even greater sense of communicative isolation than when the Myrmidons competed for our attention in lines 14-15.

In a fourth decompositional construction, suspense is generated by disrupting the decompositional process itself. In the following passage, intervening monologue between decompositional stages leaves it uncertain whether decomposition is even involved in the first place:

IL.18.1   ὣς οἳ μὲν μάρναντο δέμας πυρὸς αἰθομένοιο,

IL.18.1   So these fought on in the likeness of blazing fire. Meanwhile,

IL.18.2   Ἀντίλοχος δ' Ἀχιλῆϊ πόδας ταχὺς ἄγγελος ἦλθε.

IL.18.2   Antilochos came, a swift-footed messenger, to Achilles,

IL.18.3   τὸν δ' εὗρε προπάροιθε νεῶν ὀρθοκραιράων

IL.18.3   and found him sitting in front of the steep-horned ships, thinking

IL.18.4   τὰ φρονέοντ' ἀνὰ θυμὸν ἃ δὴ τετελεσμένα ἦεν:

IL.18.4   over in his heart of things which had now been accomplished.

In lines 5-14, Achilles delivers a soliloquy, followed by a two-stage resolution of the decompositional quandary initiated in line 3:

IL.18.15   ἕως ὃ ταῦθ' ὥρμαινε κατὰ φρένα καὶ κατὰ θυμόν,

IL.18.15   Now as he was pondering this in his heart and his spirit,

IL.18.16   τόφρά οἱ ἐγγύθεν ἦλθεν ἀγαυοῦ Νέστορος υἱὸς

IL.18.16   meanwhile the son of stately Nestor was drawing near him

IL.18.17 δάκρυα θερμά χέων, φάτο δ' ἀγγελίην ἀλεγεινήν:
IL.18.17 and wept warm tears, and gave Achilles his sorrowful message:

Although the progression from long shot to medium shot to close-up is the most common decompositional pattern in the *Iliad*, other combinations are possible as well. Sometimes these variations occur for strictly practical reasons, as when, for instance, the final stage of a series is intrinsically capacious and requires a long shot to be encompassed, as in Book 2 when Iris initiates the common descent-from-Olympus decompositional pattern:

IL.2.786 Τρωσὶν δ' ἄγγελος ἦλθε ποδήνεμος ὠκέα Ἶρις
IL.2.786 Now to the Trojans came as messenger wind-footed Iris,
IL.2.787 πὰρ Διὸς αἰγιόχοιο σὺν ἀγγελίῃ ἀλεγεινῇ:
IL.2.787 in her speed, with the dark message from Zeus of the aegis.

In the present case, however, our expectation of decompositional progress from long shot to close-up (or at least to medium shot) is thwarted by the inability of the camera to situate itself within customary range, revealing the malleable, and strictly functional, nature of the word ἀγχοῦ in line 790, which is usually reserved for contexts that express proximity between two individuals encompassed within medium shot range rather than a crowd of people within long shot range:

IL.2.788 οἳ δ' ἀγορὰς ἀγόρευον ἐπὶ Πριάμοιο θύρῃσι
IL.2.788 These were holding assembly in front of the doors of Priam
IL.2.789 πάντες ὁμηγερέες ἠμὲν νέοι ἠδὲ γέροντες:
IL.2.789 gathered together in one place, the elders and the young men.
IL.2.790 ἀγχοῦ δ' ἱσταμένη προσέφη πόδας ὠκέα Ἶρις:
IL.2.790 Standing close at hand swift-running Iris spoke to them,

Decompositional variety is not limited to practical necessity, however: it can also be used for artistic effect. Usually after the dialogue following a decompositional series, as in the four types examined above, the spatial canvas is reset and a new scene begins, unrelated to the previous construction. This sense of closure is especially prevalent when the decompositional series ends (as, for example, in the Chryses scene in lines 1.430-41) with a close-up (ἐν χερσὶ [441]) rather than merely a medium shot (Χρυσηῒς [439]), leaving no uncertainty as to its peremptory nature. In lines 446-48, for example, after Odysseus speaks to Chryses, the scene shifts to a completely new stage of action:

IL.1.446   ὣς εἰπὼν ἐν χερσὶ τίθει, ὃ δὲ δέξατο χαίρων
IL.1.446   He spoke, and left her in his arms. And he received gladly
IL.1.447   παῖδα φίλην: τοὶ δ' ὦκα θεῷ κλειτὴν ἑκατόμβην
IL.1.447   his beloved child. And the men arranged the sacred hecatomb
IL.1.448   ἑξείης ἔστησαν ἐΰδμητον περὶ βωμόν,
IL.1.448   for the god in orderly fashion around the strong-founded altar.

In the next passage under consideration, however, Homer expands a decompositional series beyond its usual limits, generating in the audience both surprise, once we realize we are still taking part in a process we thought had already been completed, and suspense, in our curiosity as to how this unexpected spatial gesture will ultimately be resolved.

In the first line of the *Iliad*, Homer establishes the theme of the epic: the wrath of Achilles. The immediate cause of this wrath is Agamemnon's insistence that, if he himself is to comply with the priest Chryses' request to hand over Chryseis to appease Apollo, then Achilles must himself hand over Briseis to Agamemnon. This request leads to a heated confrontation between the two warriors, resulting in Achilles' promise to return home rather than to prolong the war, a war which hardly concerns him personally anyway. Agamemnon accepts Achilles' resignation and Achilles retreats from the Greek camp and returns to his own shelter with his own men. In lines 321-25, Agamemnon orders the heralds Talthybios and Eurybates to retreive Briseis from Achilles, delivering on his earlier threat to him. What follows is the first decompositional series of the *Iliad*.

In lines 327-29, the heralds move progressively closer to Achilles, in three distinct stages, from an extreme long shot of the beach, a less expansive long shot of the general vicinity of Achilles, and finally a medium shot of Achilles himself who, after a few more preliminary lines, addresses the heralds:

IL.1.326   ὣς εἰπὼν προΐει, κρατερὸν δ' ἐπὶ μῦθον ἔτελλε:

IL.1.326 He spoke and sent them forth with this strong order upon them.

IL.1.327 τὼ δ' ἀέκοντε βάτην παρὰ θῖν' ἁλὸς ἀτρυγέτοιο,

IL.1.327 They went against their will beside the beach of the barren

IL.1.328 Μυρμιδόνων δ' ἐπί τε κλισίας καὶ νῆας ἱκέσθην,

IL.1.328 salt sea, and came to the shelters and the ships of the Myrmidons.

IL.1.329 τὸν δ' εὗρον παρά τε κλισίῃ καὶ νηῒ μελαίνῃ

IL.1.329 The man himself they found beside his shelter and his black ship

IL.1.330 ἥμενον· οὐδ' ἄρα τώ γε ἰδὼν γήθησεν Ἀχιλλεύς.

IL.1.330 sitting. And Achilles took no joy at all when he saw them.

As mentioned above, decomposition usually culminates at close-up rather than merely medium shot range, to focus the audience's attention on the ensuing dialogue by bringing them as close to the action as possible. The medium shot in line 329, however, leaves open the possibility for further decompositional development. Likewise, in the ensuing scene between Achilles and the heralds, Achilles' appeal for the heralds to move closer to him calls into question whether the preceding decompositional series has been completed, generating suspense as to whether the audience will penetrate even further into the action than they already have:

IL.1.334 χαίρετε κήρυκες Διὸς ἄγγελοι ἠδὲ καὶ ἀνδρῶν,

IL.1.334 'Welcome, heralds, messengers of Zeus and of mortals.

IL.1.335 ἆσσον ἴτ':

IL.1.335 Draw near.

In the next ten lines Achilles orders Patroclus to fetch Briseis from his shelter, thereby increasing the suspense. Patroclus obeys Achilles and before we know it the heralds are travelling παρὰ νῆας Ἀχαιῶν (347) to the Greek camp. Thus, despite the centripetal momentum generated by Achilles' invitation for the heralds to approach him, we suddenly revert to long shot range, which is further perpetuated by Achilles' solitary view of the wide expanse of the sea before him as he prays to Thetis. It is then, after Achilles' prayer, that the suspended resolution of the first decompositional series reveals itself as a strategic exploitation of our desire to penetrate the action which, once it occurs, strikes us all the more forceably through an extreme close-up of Achilles' tear:

IL.1.357 ὣς φάτο δάκρυ χέων, τοῦ δ' ἔκλυε πότνια μήτηρ
IL.1.357 So he spoke in tears and the lady his mother heard him

Another decompositional series follows, beginning with a long shot of Thetis emerging from the sea, a medium shot of mother and son beside each other on the shore, and a reiteration of Achilles' tears, the peremptory dramatic function of which is corroborated by a close-up of Thetis' hand, in initial position, wiping them away before she addresses her son within the rarified atmosphere created through decompositional artistry:

IL.1.358 ἡμένη ἐν βένθεσσιν ἁλὸς παρὰ πατρὶ γέροντι:
IL.1.358 as she sat in the depths of the sea at the side of her aged father,
IL.1.359 καρπαλίμως δ' ἀνέδυ πολιῆς ἁλὸς ἠΰτ' ὀμίχλη,
IL.1.359 and lightly she emerged like a mist from the grey water.
IL.1.360 καί ῥα πάροιθ' αὐτοῖο καθέζετο δάκρυ χέοντος,
IL.1.360 She came and sat beside him as he wept, and stroked him
IL.1.361 χειρί τέ μιν κατέρεξεν ἔπος τ' ἔφατ' ἔκ τ' ὀνόμαζε:
IL.1.361 with her hand and called him by name and spoke to him:

Thus, Homer inaugurates the crucial dialogue in lines 364-427 between Thetis and Achilles by prolonging the decompositional series initiated in line 327, generating more suspense, dramatic tension, and pathos than the mere transition to a completely unrelated scenographic construction after the medium shot in line 329 could have achieved.

We now turn to a device which, like decomposition, relies upon a tripartite spatial code to establish a predictable centripetality to the action that can be articulated with or without pause, depending upon whether the poet wishes to generate suspense between two or more stages of it. While the long shot, medium shot, and close-up ranges of decomposition, however, correspond to the distance of the *audience* from a given character or object to which their attention is directed, the tripartite code of the next device corresponds to the distance of *characters* from each other upon the Trojan plain.

# CHAPTER THREE

# INTERCUTTING

"Griffith arrived at montage through the method of parallel action, and he was led to the idea of parallel action by—Dickens!" (Eisenstein, 1977: 205)

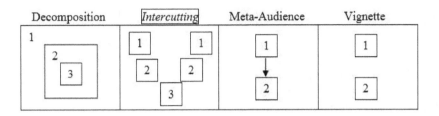

Intercutting is an editing technique that enables the filmmaker to depict simultaneous action in separate locations by alternating between them.[155] It serves as the horizontal equivalent to decomposition: the x-axis contraction of discourse spaces until they meet at a central point. Whereas decomposition involves a single mobile subject, intercutting involves two subjects located at opposite ends of a common goal. Although Münsterberg considers the device to be unique to film,[156] Homer employs it frequently in the *Iliad*, cutting between warriors on the Greek and Trojan lines of battle until they eventually engage in hand-to-hand combat. To control x-axis action with the same precision afforded by the long shot, medium shot, and close-up ranges of decomposition, Homer establishes an equivalent tripartite system to represent the three primary distances between characters when they engage in warfare on the Trojan plain: arrow-shot, spear-shot, and sword-stab.[157]

---

[155] Cf. Phillips (1999: 565); Feldman (1952: 75-7); Stern (1979: 64); Singor (1995: 191).

[156] 1970: 44-5. Cf. Feldman (1952: 78).

[157] Cf. Hainsworth (1993: 190): "Homer uses no measures of distance such as must have been in vernacular use (e.g. fingers, feet, cubits) except the πέλεθρον ([*Il.*] 21.407, *Od.* 11.577), but makes imprecise and imaginative comparisons...some of which at least appear to be traditional—'as far as a spear cast'...'as far as a man shouting can make himself heard.'"

The furthest range between two characters is represented by bow-fighting. In the following scene, Homer dramatizes, through the tension generated by tactile (123-24), sonic (125), and anthropomorphic (126) imagery, the vast distance that the arrow shot by Pandaros must travel before it finally reaches Menelaos:

IL.4.122 ἕλκε δ' ὁμοῦ γλυφίδας τε λαβὼν καὶ νεῦρα βόεια:
IL.4.122 [Pandaros] drew, holding at once the grooves and the ox-hide bowstring
IL.4.123 νευρὴν μὲν μαζῷ πέλασεν, τόξῳ δὲ σίδηρον.
IL.4.123 and brought the string against his nipple, iron to the bowstave.
IL.4.124 αὐτὰρ ἐπεὶ δὴ κυκλοτερὲς μέγα τόξον ἔτεινε,
IL.4.124 But when he had pulled the great weapon till it made a circle,
IL.4.125 λίγξε βιός, νευρὴ δὲ μέγ' ἴαχεν, ἅλτο δ' ὀϊστὸς
IL.4.125 the bow groaned, and the string sang high, and the arrow, sharp-pointed,
IL.4.126 ὀξυβελὴς καθ' ὅμιλον ἐπιπτέσθαι μενεαίνων.
IL.4.126 leapt away, furious, to fly through the throng before it.

Just as the long shot of a deity descending from Olympus to find a mortal on the Trojan plain prepares the audience to move closer to the object of this search, so when characters stand at arrow-shot distance from each other a similar anticipation to get within spear-shot is generated, as when Diomedes is within arrow-shot of Pandaros in Book 5:

IL.5.114 δὴ τότ' ἔπειτ' ἠρᾶτο βοὴν ἀγαθὸς Διομήδης:
IL.5.114 Now Diomedes of the great war cry spoke aloud, praying:
IL.5.115 κλῦθί μοι αἰγιόχοιο Διὸς τέκος Ἀτρυτώνη,
IL.5.115 'Hear me now, Atrytone, daughter of Zeus of the aegis:
IL.5.116 εἴ ποτέ μοι καὶ πατρὶ φίλα φρονέουσα παρέστης
IL.5.116 if ever before in kindliness you stood by my father
IL.5.117 δηΐῳ ἐν πολέμῳ, νῦν αὖτ' ἐμὲ φῖλαι Ἀθήνη:
IL.5.117 through the terror of fighting, be my friend now also, Athene;
IL.5.118 δὸς δέ τέ μ' ἄνδρα ἑλεῖν καὶ ἐς ὁρμὴν ἔγχεος ἐλθεῖν
IL.5.118 grant me that I may kill this man and come within spearcast,
IL.5.119 ὅς μ' ἔβαλε φθάμενος καὶ ἐπεύχεται, οὐδέ μέ φησι
IL.5.119 who shot me before I could see him, and now boasts over me, saying
IL.5.120 δηρὸν ἔτ' ὄψεσθαι λαμπρὸν φάος ἠελίοιο.
IL.5.120 I cannot live to look much longer on the shining sunlight.'

And when Pandaros fails to hit Diomedes with his arrow, he too expresses his intention to get within spear-shot range of his adversary:

IL.5.276 τὸν πρότερος προσέειπε Λυκάονος ἀγλαὸς υἱός:

IL.5.276   First to Diomedes called out the shining son of Lykaon:
IL.5.277   καρτερόθυμε δαΐφρον ἀγαυοῦ Τυδέος υἱὲ
IL.5.277   'Valiant and strong-spirited, o son of proud Tydeus,
IL.5.278   ἦ μάλα σ' οὐ βέλος ὠκὺ δαμάσσατο πικρὸς ὀϊστός:
IL.5.278   you were not beaten then by the bitter arrow, my swift shot.
IL.5.279   νῦν αὖτ' ἐγχείῃ πειρήσομαι αἴ κε τύχωμι.
IL.5.279   Now I will try with the throwing-spear to see if I can hit you.'

The next range between two characters on the Trojan plain is represented by spear-fighting. Just as the medium shot serves in an intermediary capacity in decomposition, spanning medium long shot to medium close-up ranges, so the spear shot exhibits a similar versatility. Sometimes, for example, spears and stones (another common *sema* of spear-shot distance) are used interchangeably with arrows, when the contrast between arrow-shot and spear-shot ranges is not emphasized:

IL.16.772   πολλὰ δὲ Κεβριόνην ἀμφ' ὀξέα δοῦρα πεπήγει
IL.16.772   and many sharp spears were driven home about Kebriones
IL.16.773   ἰοί τε πτερόεντες ἀπὸ νευρῆφι θορόντες,
IL.16.773   and many feathered arrows sprung from the bowstrings, many
IL.16.774   πολλὰ δὲ χερμάδια μεγάλ' ἀσπίδας ἐστυφέλιξαν
IL.16.774   great throwing stones pounded against the shields

When this contrast is central to a scene, however, spear-fighting is clearly differentiated from bow-fighting, representing the kinds of warfare one engages in from far away (ἑκὰς):

IL.13.259   τὸν δ' αὖτ' Ἰδομενεὺς Κρητῶν ἀγὸς ἀντίον ηὔδα:
IL.13.259   Then Idomeneus lord of the Kretans answered him in turn:
IL.13.260   δούρατα δ' αἴ κ' ἐθέλῃσθα καὶ ἓν καὶ εἴκοσι δήεις
IL.13.260   'You will find one spear, and twenty spears, if you want them,
IL.13.261   ἑσταότ' ἐν κλισίῃ πρὸς ἐνώπια παμφανόωντα
IL.13.261   standing against the shining inward wall in my shelter,
IL.13.262   Τρώϊα, τὰ κταμένων ἀποαίνυμαι: οὐ γὰρ ὀΐω
IL.13.262   Trojan spears I win from men that I kill, for my way
IL.13.263   ἀνδρῶν δυσμενέων ἑκὰς ἱστάμενος πολεμίζειν.
IL.13.263   is not to fight my battles standing far away from my enemies.
IL.13.264   τώ μοι δούρατά τ' ἔστι καὶ ἀσπίδες ὀμφαλόεσσαι
IL.13.264   Thereby I have spears there, and shields massive in the middle,
IL.13.265   καὶ κόρυθες καὶ θώρηκες λαμπρὸν γανόωντες.
IL.13.265   and helms and corselets are there in all the pride of their shining.'

63

At the other extreme, spears can be used in conjunction with swords at close enough range from one victim to get within sword-stab range of another without missing a beat:

IL.5.144 ἔνθ' ἕλεν Ἀστύνοον καὶ Ὑπείρονα ποιμένα λαῶν,
IL.5.144 Next he killed Astynoös and Hypeiron, shepherd of the people,
IL.5.145 τὸν μὲν ὑπὲρ μαζοῖο βαλὼν χαλκήρεϊ δουρί,
IL.5.145 striking one with the bronze-heeled spear above the nipple,
IL.5.146 τὸν δ' ἕτερον ξίφεϊ μεγάλῳ κληῖδα παρ' ὦμον
IL.5.146 and cutting the other beside the shoulder through the collar-bone
IL.5.147 πλῆξ', ἀπὸ δ' αὐχένος ὦμον ἐέργαθεν ἠδ' ἀπὸ νώτου.
IL.5.147 with the great sword, so that neck and back were hewn free of the shoulder.

In fact, spears can also be used interchangeably with swords, serving as stabbing rather than throwing weapons,

IL.13.146 στῆ ῥα μάλ' ἐγχριμφθείς: οἳ δ' ἀντίοι υἷες Ἀχαιῶν
IL.13.146 he was stopped, hard, beaten in on himself. The sons of the Achaians
IL.13.147 νύσσοντες ξίφεσίν τε καὶ ἔγχεσιν ἀμφιγύοισιν
IL.13.147 against him stabbing at him with swords and leaf-headed spears
IL.13.148 ὦσαν ἀπὸ σφείων: ὃ δὲ χασσάμενος πελεμίχθη.
IL.13.148 thrust him away from them so that he gave ground backward, staggering.

or in conjunction with swords, to underscore a warrior's surrealistic ability to range simultaneously over two distant stretches of the Trojan plain:

IL.20.460 αὐτὰρ ὃ Λαόγονον καὶ Δάρδανον υἷε Βίαντος
IL.20.460 Then Achilles swooping on Dardanos and Laogonos, sons both
IL.20.461 ἄμφω ἐφορμηθεὶς ἐξ ἵππων ὦσε χαμᾶζε,
IL.20.461 of Bias, dashed them to the ground from behind their horses,
IL.20.462 τὸν μὲν δουρὶ βαλών, τὸν δὲ σχεδὸν ἄορι τύψας.
IL.20.462 one with a spearcast, one with a stroke of the sword from close up.

This dual function of spears is corroborated diegetically as well, in Priam's explicit contrast between their two primary uses in Book 22,

IL.22.66 αὐτὸν δ' ἂν πύματόν με κύνες πρώτῃσι θύρῃσιν
IL.22.66 And myself last of all, my dogs in front of my doorway
IL.22.67 ὠμησταὶ ἐρύουσιν, ἐπεί κέ τις ὀξέϊ χαλκῷ
IL.22.67 will rip me raw, after some man with stroke of the sharp bronze

64

IL.22.68   τύψας ἠὲ βαλὼν ῥεθέων ἐκ θυμὸν ἕληται,
IL.22.68   spear, or with spearcast, has torn the life out of my body;

as well as by the fact that the lemma ἐγγύς, meaning "close," can represent either spear-shot or sword-stab distance, depending upon the context. In this scene from the chariot games of Patroclus in Book 23, for example, we are not sure what is meant by ἐγγύθεν until the simile in lines 517-23 establishes sword-stab distance between Menelaos and Antilochos:

IL.23.514   τῷ δ' ἄρ' ἐπ' Ἀντίλοχος Νηλήϊος ἤλασεν ἵππους
IL.23.514   After him Neleian Antilochos drove in his horses,
IL.23.515   κέρδεσιν, οὔ τι τάχει γε, παραφθάμενος Μενέλαον:
IL.23.515   having passed Menelaos, not by speed but by taking advantage.
IL.23.516   ἀλλὰ καὶ ὣς Μενέλαος ἔχ' ἐγγύθεν ὠκέας ἵππους.
IL.23.516   But even so Menelaos held his fast horses close on him.
IL.23.517   ὅσσον δὲ τροχοῦ ἵππος ἀφίσταται, ὅς ῥα τ' ἄνακτα
IL.23.517   As far as from the wheel stands the horse who is straining
IL.23.518   ἕλκῃσιν πεδίοιο τιταινόμενος σὺν ὄχεσφι:
IL.23.518   to pull his master with the chariot over the flat land;
IL.23.519   τοῦ μέν τε ψαύουσιν ἐπισσώτρου τρίχες ἄκραι
IL.23.519   the extreme hairs in the tail of the horse brush against the running
IL.23.520   οὐραῖαι: ὃ δέ τ' ἄγχι μάλα τρέχει, οὐδέ τι πολλὴ
IL.23.520   rim of the wheel, and he courses very close, there is not much
IL.23.521   χώρη μεσσηγὺς πολέος πεδίοιο θέοντος:
IL.23.521   space between as he runs a great way over the flat land;
IL.23.522   τόσσον δὴ Μενέλαος ἀμύμονος Ἀντιλόχοιο
IL.23.522   by so much Menelaos by Antilochos the blameless
IL.23.523   λείπετ'.
IL.23.523   was left behind.

In line 219 of Book 7, on the other hand, Ajax is said to come ἐγγύθεν to Hector:

IL.7.219   Αἴας δ' ἐγγύθεν ἦλθε φέρων σάκος ἠΰτε πύργον
IL.7.219   Now Aias came near him, carrying like a wall his shield

After a description of Ajax's shield in lines 220-23, Homer reiterates the "closeness" between the two warriors:

65

IL.7.225    στῆ ῥα μάλ' Ἕκτορος ἐγγύς, ἀπειλήσας δὲ προσηύδα:
IL.7.225    [Ajax] stood near Hektor and spoke to him in words of menace:

This use of ἐγγύς, however, brings us no closer to ascertaining whether Ajax and Hector are within spear-shot or sword-stab range of each other. For the next eighteen lines, they exchange words, until finally, in line 244, Ajax throws a spear at Hector,

IL.7.244    ἦ ῥα, καὶ ἀμπεπαλὼν προΐει δολιχόσκιον ἔγχος,
IL.7.244    So he spoke, and balanced the spear far-shadowed, and threw it,

retrospectively establishing the spear-shot rather than sword-stab range between the two warriors during their intervening dialogue.

The closest distance between two characters on the Trojan plain is represented by sword-fighting. When characters stand at spear-shot range from each other we expect them to proceed to sword-stab range.[158] In a common scenario, two characters exchange spear throws without killing each other, inducing them to approach each other further and to engage in hand-to-hand combat at sword-stab range. In the duel between Menelaos and Paris in Book 3, for example, Paris throws a spear at Menelaos,

IL.3.346    πρόσθε δ' Ἀλέξανδρος προΐει δολιχόσκιον ἔγχος,
IL.3.346    First of the two Alexandros let go his spear far-shadowing

and hits his shield,

IL.3.347    καὶ βάλεν Ἀτρεΐδαο κατ' ἀσπίδα πάντοσ' ἐΐσην,
IL.3.347    and struck the shield of Atreus' son on its perfect circle

yet without doing damage:

IL.3.348    οὐδ' ἔρρηξεν χαλκόν, ἀνεγνάμφθη δέ οἱ αἰχμὴ
IL.3.348    nor did the bronze point break its way through, but the spearhead bent back
IL.3.349    ἀσπίδι ἐνὶ κρατερῇ:

---

[158] Lines 707-12 of Book 15 illustrate the teleological nature of x-axis war-fare, the natural progression from bow- and spear-fighting to sword-fighting.

IL.3.349  in the strong shield.

We now expect Menelaos to reciprocate, and Homer obliges. Menelaos throws a spear at Paris,

IL.3.355  ἦ ῥα καὶ ἀμπεπαλὼν προΐει δολιχόσκιον ἔγχος,
IL.3.355  So he spoke, and balanced the spear far-shadowed, and threw it
IL.3.356  καὶ βάλε Πριαμίδαο κατ' ἀσπίδα πάντοσ' ἐΐσην:
IL.3.356  and struck the shield of Priam's son on its perfect circle.

which, although the graphic details of the spear's trajectory in lines 358-59 produces more suspense than the cursory description of Paris' spear in lines 348-49,

IL.3.357  διὰ μὲν ἀσπίδος ἦλθε φαεινῆς ὄβριμον ἔγχος,
IL.3.357  All the way through the glittering shield went the heavy spearhead
IL.3.358  καὶ διὰ θώρηκος πολυδαιδάλου ἠρήρειστο:
IL.3.358  and smashed its way through the intricately worked corselet;
IL.3.359  ἀντικρὺ δὲ παραὶ λαπάρην διάμησε χιτῶνα
IL.3.359  straight ahead by the flank the spearhead shore through his tunic,

is no more successful at wounding its target.

IL.3.360  ἔγχος: ὃ δ' ἐκλίνθη καὶ ἀλεύατο κῆρα μέλαιναν.
IL.3.360  yet he bent away to one side and avoided the dark death.

We now expect the characters to progress to sword-stab range from each other, as indeed they do, until Aphrodite rescues Paris in line 380 and removes him from the fray, in a variety of the *deus ex machina* device that occurs when key characters reach the end of an intercutting series but are too crucial to the plot to be killed off:[159]

IL.3.380  ἔγχεϊ χαλκείῳ: τὸν δ' ἐξήρπαξ' Ἀφροδίτη
IL.3.380  with the bronze spear. But Aphrodite caught up Paris
IL.3.381  ῥεῖα μάλ' ὥς τε θεός, ἐκάλυψε δ' ἄρ' ἠέρι πολλῇ,

---

[159] On the other hand, when the victim is a minor character, as in the scene between Achilles and Asteropaios in lines 161-83, for example, he frequently ends up being killed, thus fulfilling the intercutting series, precluding the resort to diversionary tactics, and occasioning a fresh change of scene.

IL.3.381   easily, since she was divine, and wrapped him in a thick mist
IL.3.382   κὰδ δ' εἶσ' ἐν θαλάμῳ εὐώδεϊ κηώεντι.
IL.3.382   and set him down again in his own perfumed bedchamber.

In an abbreviated version of this progression from spear-shot to sword-stab range, Agamemnon throws a spear at one character and then stabs another:

IL.11.107   δὴ τότε γ' Ἀτρείδης εὐρὺ κρείων Ἀγαμέμνων
IL.11.107   This time the son of Atreus, wide-powerful Agamemnon,
IL.11.108   τὸν μὲν ὑπὲρ μαζοῖο κατὰ στῆθος βάλε δουρί,
IL.11.108   struck Isos with the thrown spear in the chest above the nipple
IL.11.109   Ἄντιφον αὖ παρὰ οὖς ἔλασε ξίφει, ἐκ δ' ἔβαλ' ἵππων.
IL.11.109   and hit Antiphos by the ear with the sword and hurled him from his horses,

The rapid succession of these actions emphasizes the military prowess of Agamemnon, a tendency that is further exploited when Homer uses the phrase ἔγχεΐ τ' ἄορί τε μεγάλοισί τε χερμαδίοισιν to represent the ubiquitousness of Agamemnon

IL.11.264   αὐτὰρ ὃ τῶν ἄλλων ἐπεπωλεῖτο στίχας ἀνδρῶν
IL.11.264   But Agamemnon ranged the ranks of the other fighters
IL.11.265   ἔγχεΐ τ' ἄορί τε μεγάλοισί τε χερμαδίοισιν,
IL.11.265   with spear and sword and with huge stones that he flung, for such time
IL.11.266   ὄφρά οἱ αἶμ' ἔτι θερμὸν ἀνήνοθεν ἐξ ὠτειλῆς.
IL.11.266   as the blood was still running warm from the spear-wound.

and Hector:

IL.11.537   αἵ τ' ἀπ' ἐπισσώτρων. ὃ δὲ ἵετο δῦναι ὅμιλον
IL.11.537   from the running rims of the wheels. So Hektor was straining to plunge in
IL.11.538   ἀνδρόμεον ῥῆξαί τε μετάλμενος: ἐν δὲ κυδοιμὸν
IL.11.538   the turmoil of men, and charge them and break them. He hurled the confusion
IL.11.539   ἧκε κακὸν Δαναοῖσι, μίνυνθα δὲ χάζετο δουρός.
IL.11.539   of disaster upon the Danaans, and stayed from the spear's stroke
IL.11.540   αὐτὰρ ὃ τῶν ἄλλων ἐπεπωλεῖτο στίχας ἀνδρῶν
IL.11.540   little, but ranged about among the ranks of the rest of the fighters
IL.11.541   ἔγχεΐ τ' ἄορί τε μεγάλοισί τε χερμαδίοισιν,
IL.11.541   with his spear and his sword and with huge stones flung,
IL.11.542   Αἴαντος δ' ἀλέεινε μάχην Τελαμωνιάδαο.
IL.11.542   yet kept clear still of the attack of Telamonian Aias.

The three x-axis distances represent distinct ethical qualities in the

*Iliad*: there are specific emotions associated with long- and short-range fighting. To begin with, the archer is stigmatized as a coward:

IL.11.384 τὸν δ' οὐ ταρβήσας προσέφη κρατερὸς Διομήδης:
IL.11.384 Then not at all frightened strong Diomedes answered him:
IL.11.385 τοξότα λωβητὴρ κέρᾳ ἀγλαὲ παρθενοπῖπα
IL.11.385 'You archer, foul fighter, lovely in your locks, eyer of young girls.
IL.11.386 εἰ μὲν δὴ ἀντίβιον σὺν τεύχεσι πειρηθείης,
IL.11.386 If you were to make trial of me in strong combat with weapons
IL.11.387 οὐκ ἄν τοι χραίσμῃσι βιὸς καὶ ταρφέες ἰοί:
IL.11.387 your bow would do you no good at all, nor your close-showered arrows.
IL.11.388 νῦν δέ μ' ἐπιγράψας ταρσὸν ποδὸς εὔχεαι αὔτως.
IL.11.388 Now you have scratched the flat of my foot, and even boast of this.
IL.11.389 οὐκ ἀλέγω, ὡς εἴ με γυνὴ βάλοι ἢ πάϊς ἄφρων:
IL.11.389 I care no more than if a witless child or a woman
IL.11.390 κωφὸν γὰρ βέλος ἀνδρὸς ἀνάλκιδος οὐτιδανοῖο.
IL.11.390 had struck me; this is the blank weapon of a useless man, no fighter.

The close-range fighter, on the other hand, is courageous, daring to look his enemy in the eyes:

IL.17.164 τοίου γὰρ θεράπων πέφατ' ἀνέρος, ὃς μέγ' ἄριστος
IL.17.164 Such is the man whose henchman is killed. He is far the greatest
IL.17.165 Ἀργείων παρὰ νηυσὶ καὶ ἀγχέμαχοι θεράποντες.
IL.17.165 of the Argives by the ships, and his men fight hard at close quarters.
IL.17.166 ἀλλὰ σύ γ' Αἴαντος μεγαλήτορος οὐκ ἐτάλασσας
IL.17.166 No, but you could not bring yourself to stand up against Aias
IL.17.167 στήμεναι ἄντα κατ' ὄσσε ἰδὼν δηΐων ἐν αὐτῇ,
IL.17.167 of the great heart, nor to look at his eyes in the clamour of fighting
IL.17.168 οὐδ' ἰθὺς μαχέσασθαι, ἐπεὶ σέο φέρτερός ἐστι.
IL.17.168 men, nor attack him direct, since he is far better than you are.'

This is corroborated by the following simile, in which the close-fighter is compared to a lion, whom others fear to engage at sword stab range:

IL.17.61 ὡς δ' ὅτε τίς τε λέων ὀρεσίτροφος ἀλκὶ πεποιθὼς
IL.17.61 As when in the confidence of his strength some lion
IL.17.62 βοσκομένης ἀγέλης βοῦν ἁρπάσῃ ἥ τις ἀρίστη:
IL.17.62 hill-reared snatches the finest cow in a herd as it pastures;
IL.17.63 τῆς δ' ἐξ αὐχέν' ἔαξε λαβὼν κρατεροῖσιν ὀδοῦσι
IL.17.63 first the lion breaks her neck caught fast in the strong teeth,
IL.17.64 πρῶτον, ἔπειτα δέ θ' αἷμα καὶ ἔγκατα πάντα λαφύσσει

IL.17.64  then gulps down the blood and all the guts that are inward
IL.17.65  δηῶν: ἀμφὶ δὲ τόν γε κύνες ἄνδρές τε νομῆες
IL.17.65  savagely, as the dogs and the herdsmen raise a commotion
IL.17.66  πολλὰ μάλ' ἰύζουσιν ἀπόπροθεν οὐδ' ἐθέλουσιν
IL.17.66  loudly about him, but from a distance, and are not willing
IL.17.67  ἀντίον ἐλθέμεναι: μάλα γὰρ χλωρὸν δέος αἱρεῖ:
IL.17.67  to go in and face him, since the hard green fear has hold of them;
IL.17.68  ὣς τῶν οὔ τινι θυμὸς ἐνὶ στήθεσσιν ἐτόλμα
IL.17.68  so no heart in the breast of any Trojan had courage
IL.17.69  ἀντίον ἐλθέμεναι Μενελάου κυδαλίμοιο.
IL.17.69  to go in and face glorious Menelaos.

Just as the progression from long shot to close-up in a decompositional series can be delayed to generate suspense, so the intercutting equivalent can occur. This is achieved by shifting the focus of attention temporarily from the centripetal merging of frames to dialogue, as in the following scene between Tlepolemos and Sarpedon in Book 5. In lines 628-29, an impending duel between the two warriors is established:

IL.5.628  Τληπόλεμον δ' Ἡρακλεΐδην ἠΰν τε μέγαν τε
IL.5.628  But Herakles' son Tlepolemos the huge and mighty
IL.5.629  ὦρσεν ἐπ' ἀντιθέῳ Σαρπηδόνι μοῖρα κραταιή.
IL.5.629  was driven by his strong destiny against godlike Sarpedon.

This leads us to expect them to approach each other, as they in fact do in the next two lines:

IL.5.630  οἳ δ' ὅτε δὴ σχεδὸν ἦσαν ἐπ' ἀλλήλοισιν ἰόντες
IL.5.630  Now as these in their advance had come close together,
IL.5.631  υἱός θ' υἱωνός τε Διὸς νεφεληγερέταο,
IL.5.631  the own son, and the son's son of Zeus cloud-gathering,

Yet rather than immediately consummate this development, the characters suddenly engage in dialogue:

IL.5.632  τὸν καὶ Τληπόλεμος πρότερος πρὸς μῦθον ἔειπε:
IL.5.632  it was Tlepolemos of the two who spoke the first word:

IL.5.647    τὸν δ' αὖ Σαρπηδὼν Λυκίων ἀγὸς ἀντίον ηὔδα:
IL.5.647    In turn the lord of the Lykians, Sarpedon, answered him:


It is not until lines 655-59 that the centripetal momentum generated in lines 628-30 is resumed and resolved:

IL.5.655    ὣς φάτο Σαρπηδών, ὃ δ' ἀνέσχετο μείλινον ἔγχος
IL.5.655    So spoke Sarpedon, while the other lifted his ash spear,
IL.5.656    Τληπόλεμος· καὶ τῶν μὲν ἁμαρτῇ δούρατα μακρὰ
IL.5.656    Tlepolemos; and in a single moment the long shafts
IL.5.657    ἐκ χειρῶν ἤϊξαν: ὃ μὲν βάλεν αὐχένα μέσσον
IL.5.657    shot from their hands, Sarpedon striking him in the middle
IL.5.658    Σαρπηδών, αἰχμὴ δὲ διαμπερὲς ἦλθ' ἀλεγεινή:
IL.5.658    of the throat, and the agonizing spear drove clean through
IL.5.659    τὸν δὲ κατ' ὀφθαλμῶν ἐρεβεννὴ νὺξ ἐκάλυψε.
IL.5.659    and over his eyes was mantled the covering mist of darkness.

An intercutting series, like its decompositional counterpart, can also be aborted rather than merely delayed. As in the first instance of decomposition—when the heralds obey Agamemnon's order to find Achilles near his shelter in Book 1—the first instance of intercutting in the *Iliad* is prematurely terminated, thwarting the apparently inevitable contraction of Greek and Trojan lines of battle. We first get an establishing shot[160] of both lines of battle:

IL.3.1    αὐτὰρ ἐπεὶ κόσμηθεν ἅμ' ἡγεμόνεσσιν ἕκαστοι,
IL.3.1    Now when the men of both sides were set in order by their leaders,

Then each side is introduced individually, by means of a simile. The Trojans are compared to noisy birds,

IL.3.2    Τρῶες μὲν κλαγγῇ τ' ἐνοπῇ τ' ἴσαν ὄρνιθες ὣς
IL.3.2    the Trojans came on with clamour and shouting, like wildfowl,

while the Greeks proceed silently:

IL.3.8    οἳ δ' ἄρ' ἴσαν σιγῇ μένεα πνείοντες Ἀχαιοὶ

---

[160] Cf. Phillips (1999: 567).

71

IL.3.8   But the Achaian men went silently, breathing valour,

IL.3.9   ἐν θυμῷ μεμαῶτες ἀλεξέμεν ἀλλήλοισιν.

IL.3.9   stubbornly minded each in his heart to stand by the others.

Then Homer increases the tension of the imminent encounter of the two armies through another simile, emphasizing the commotion of the scene,

IL.3.10   εὖτ' ὄρεος κορυφῇσι Νότος κατέχευεν ὀμίχλην

IL.3.10   As on the peaks of a mountain the south wind scatters the thick mist,

IL.3.11   ποιμέσιν οὔ τι φίλην, κλέπτῃ δέ τε νυκτὸς ἀμείνω,

IL.3.11   no friend to the shepherd, but better than night for the robber,

IL.3.12   τόσσόν τίς τ' ἐπιλεύσσει ὅσον τ' ἐπὶ λᾶαν ἵησιν:

IL.3.12   and a man can see before him only so far as a stone cast,

IL.3.13   ὣς ἄρα τῶν ὑπὸ ποσσὶ κονίσαλος ὤρνυτ' ἀελλὴς

IL.3.13   so beneath their feet the dust drove up in a stormcloud

IL.3.14   ἐρχομένων: μάλα δ' ὦκα διέπρησσον πεδίοιο.

IL.3.14   of men marching, who made their way through the plain in great speed.

followed by the formula

IL.3.15   οἳ δ' ὅτε δὴ σχεδὸν ἦσαν ἐπ' ἀλλήλοισιν ἰόντες,

IL.3.15   Now as these in their advance had come close together,

As in 5.630 above, this line leads us to expect immediate contact between the two armies.[161] In this case, however, suspense is generated by having one warrior, Paris, advance before the rest of the Trojans and challenge any Greek to a duel:

IL.3.16   Τρωσὶν μὲν προμάχιζεν Ἀλέξανδρος θεοειδὴς

IL.3.16   Alexandros the godlike leapt from the ranks of the Trojans,

IL.3.17   παρδαλέην ὤμοισιν ἔχων καὶ καμπύλα τόξα

IL.3.17   as challenger wearing across his shoulders the hide of a leopard,

IL.3.18   καὶ ξίφος: αὐτὰρ ὁ δοῦρε δύω κεκορυθμένα χαλκῷ

IL.3.18   curved bow and sword; while in his hands shaking two javelins

IL.3.19   πάλλων Ἀργείων προκαλίζετο πάντας ἀρίστους

IL.3.19   pointed with bronze, he challenged all the best of the Argives

IL.3.20   ἀντίβιον μαχέσασθαι ἐν αἰνῇ δηϊοτῆτι.

IL.3.20   to fight man to man against him in bitter combat.

---

[161] Cf. *Il.* 5.14-15.

This sudden cut to the Trojan side is reciprocated by a cut to Menelaos,

IL.3.21  τὸν δ' ὡς οὖν ἐνόησεν ἀρηΐφιλος Μενέλαος
IL.3.21  Now as soon as Menelaos the warlike caught sight of him

through whose vision we see Paris, who appears to him as a deer to a lion:

IL.3.22  ἐρχόμενον προπάροιθεν ὁμίλου μακρὰ βιβῶντα,
IL.3.22  making his way with long strides out in front of the army,
IL.3.23  ὥς τε λέων ἐχάρη μεγάλῳ ἐπὶ σώματι κύρσας
IL.3.23  he was glad, like a lion who comes on a mighty carcass,
IL.3.24  εὑρὼν ἢ ἔλαφον κεραὸν ἢ ἄγριον αἶγα
IL.3.24  in his hunger chancing upon the body of a horned stag
IL.3.25  πεινάων: μάλα γάρ τε κατεσθίει, εἴ περ ἂν αὐτὸν
IL.3.25  or wild goat; who eats it eagerly, although against him
IL.3.26  σεύωνται ταχέες τε κύνες θαλεροί τ' αἰζηοί:
IL.3.26  are hastening the hounds in their speed and the stalwart young men:
IL.3.27  ὣς ἐχάρη Μενέλαος Ἀλέξανδρον θεοειδέα
IL.3.27  thus Menelaos was happy finding godlike Alexandros
IL.3.28  ὀφθαλμοῖσιν ἰδών: φάτο γὰρ τίσασθαι ἀλείτην:
IL.3.28  there in front of his eyes, and thinking to punish the robber,
IL.3.29  αὐτίκα δ' ἐξ ὀχέων σὺν τεύχεσιν ἆλτο χαμᾶζε.
IL.3.29  straightway in all his armour he sprang to the ground from his chariot.

This symmetrical alternation between Greek and Trojan sides is continued with a cut to Paris, through whose eyes we now see Menelaos:

IL.3.30  τὸν δ' ὡς οὖν ἐνόησεν Ἀλέξανδρος θεοειδὴς
IL.3.30  But Alexandros the godlike when he saw Menelaos
IL.3.31  ἐν προμάχοισι φανέντα,
IL.3.31  showing among the champions,

Thus, the action has proceeded in six stages up to this point: 1) extreme long shot of Greek and Trojan sides, 2) long shot of Trojan side, 3) long shot of Greek side, 4) long shot of both sides as they approach each other, 5) medium shot of Paris, 6) medium shot of Menelaos looking at Paris, and 7) medium shot of Paris looking at Menelaos. Now we expect the two warriors to engage in spear-fighting or, after drawing closer to each other through intercutting, sword-fighting. What happens instead, however, at first surprises us. Paris retreats from Menelaos,

IL.3.31 κατεπλήγη φίλον ἦτορ,
IL.3.31 the heart was shaken within [Paris];
IL.3.32 ἂψ δ' ἑτάρων εἰς ἔθνος ἐχάζετο κῆρ' ἀλεείνων.
IL.3.32 to avoid death he shrank into the host of his own companions.

like one who has been frightened away by a snake:

IL.3.33 ὡς δ' ὅτε τίς τε δράκοντα ἰδὼν παλίνορσος ἀπέστη
IL.3.33 As a man who has come on a snake in the mountain valley
IL.3.34 οὔρεος ἐν βήσσῃς, ὑπό τε τρόμος ἔλλαβε γυῖα,
IL.3.34 suddenly steps back, and the shivers come over his body,
IL.3.35 ἂψ δ' ἀνεχώρησεν, ὦχρός τέ μιν εἷλε παρειάς,
IL.3.35 and he draws back and away, cheeks seized with a green pallor;
IL.3.36 ὣς αὖτις καθ' ὅμιλον ἔδυ Τρώων ἀγερώχων
IL.3.36 so in terror of Atreus' son godlike Alexandros
IL.3.37 δείσας Ἀτρέος υἱὸν Ἀλέξανδρος θεοειδής.
IL.3.37 lost himself again in the host of the haughty Trojans.

In the previous book, however, we encountered a simile that, in retrospect, makes this development somewhat more predictable, comparing the long-distance fighter to a frightened deer:

IL.4.242 Ἀργεῖοι ἰόμωροι ἐλεγχέες οὔ νυ σέβεσθε;
IL.4.242 'Argives, you arrow-fighters, have you no shame, you abuses?
IL.4.243 τίφθ' οὕτως ἔστητε τεθηπότες ἠΰτε νεβροί,
IL.4.243 Why are you simply standing there bewildered, like young deer
IL.4.244 αἵ τ' ἐπεὶ οὖν ἔκαμον πολέος πεδίοιο θέουσαι
IL.4.244 who after they are tired from running through a great meadow
IL.4.245 ἑστᾶσ', οὐδ' ἄρα τίς σφι μετὰ φρεσὶ γίνεται ἀλκή:
IL.4.245 stand there still, and there is no heart of courage within them?

This symbolism is especially appropriate, considering the fact that Paris is known more for his bow-fighting than his sword-fighting.[162] Thus, while through framing we have been led to expect the clash of Menelaos and Paris, this simile lends thematic corroboration to Homer's choice to

---

[162] Cf. 11.385-88.

take his audience in another direction.

The following scene, on the other hand, disrupts intercutting protocol for strictly practical reasons. Although the progression from spear-shot to sword-stab range is aborted here as in the scene above, in this case it involves Homer in an inconsistency. In line 244, Hector throws a spear at Ajax,

IL.7.244 ἦ ῥα, καὶ ἀμπεπαλὼν προΐει δολιχόσκιον ἔγχος,
IL.7.244 So he spoke, and balanced the spear far-shadowed, and threw it,

and in line 249 Ajax throws a spear at Hector.

IL.7.249 Αἴας διογενὴς προΐει δολιχόσκιον ἔγχος,
IL.7.249 Ajax the illustrious in turn cast with his spear far-shadowing

Then the action progresses to sword-stab range when Hector stabs Ajax in line 258,

IL.7.258 Πριαμίδης μὲν ἔπειτα μέσον σάκος οὔτασε δουρί,
IL.7.258 Priam stabbed then with his spear into the shield's centre,

and Ajax stabs Hector in line 260:

IL.7.260 Αἴας δ' ἀσπίδα νύξεν ἐπάλμενος:
IL.7.260 Now Aias plunging upon him thrust at the shield,

So far the action has proceded according to protocol. Now that the two warriors are within sword-stab range of each other, we expect either a conclusion to their battle or some turn of events to get them out of harm's way of each other (such as when Athena rescues Paris in lines 379-82 of Book 3). Homer chooses the latter option: he brings the Greek and Trojan heralds onto the scene to shift our attention to them. He cannot do so, however, if Ajax and Hector are fighting hand-to-hand when they arrive, for they would be too embroiled with each other to notice them. Thus, to prepare for the arrival of the heralds, Homer retraces his steps: despite the sword-stab distance between Ajax and

## Hector established in line 249, Homer has Hector throw a stone at Ajax,

IL.7.263   ἀλλ' οὐδ' ὣς ἀπέληγε μάχης κορυθαίολος Ἕκτωρ,
IL.7.263   Yet even so Hektor of the shining helmet did not stop fighting,
IL.7.264   ἀλλ' ἀναχασσάμενος λίθον εἵλετο χειρὶ παχείῃ
IL.7.264   but gave back and in his heavy hand caught up a stone that
IL.7.265   κείμενον ἐν πεδίῳ μέλανα τρηχύν τε μέγαν τε:
IL.7.265   lay in the plain, black and rugged and huge. With this
IL.7.266   τῷ βάλεν Αἴαντος δεινὸν σάκος ἑπταβόειον
IL.7.266   he struck the sevenfold-ox-hide terrible shield of Aias
IL.7.267   μέσσον ἐπομφάλιον: περιήχησεν δ' ἄρα χαλκός.
IL.7.267   in the knob of the centre so that the bronze clashed loud about it.

## and has Ajax throw a stone at Hector:

IL.7.268   δεύτερος αὖτ' Αἴας πολὺ μείζονα λᾶαν ἀείρας
IL.7.268   After him Aias in turn lifting a stone far greater
IL.7.269   ἧκ' ἐπιδινήσας, ἐπέρεισε δὲ ἶν' ἀπέλεθρον,
IL.7.269   whirled it and threw, leaning into the cast his strength beyond measure,

## Homer emphasizes this new distance between Ajax and Hector by using the clause

IL.7.273   καί νύ κε δὴ ξιφέεσσ' αὐτοσχεδὸν οὐτάζοντο,
IL.7.273   And now they would have been stabbing with their swords at close quarters,

## to clear the way for the heralds to enter the stage

IL.7.274   εἰ μὴ κήρυκες Διὸς ἄγγελοι ἠδὲ καὶ ἀνδρῶν
IL.7.274   had not the heralds, messengers of Zeus and of mortals,
IL.7.275   ἦλθον, ὃ μὲν Τρώων, ὃ δ' Ἀχαιῶν χαλκοχιτώνων,
IL.7.275   come up, one for the bronze-armoured Achaians, one for the Trojans,
IL.7.276   Ταλθύβιός τε καὶ Ἰδαῖος πεπνυμένω ἄμφω:
IL.7.276   Idaios and Talthybios, both men of good counsel.

## and to urge the two warriors to strike a temporary truce:

IL.7.277   μέσσῳ δ' ἀμφοτέρων σκῆπτρα σχέθον, εἶπέ τε μῦθον
IL.7.277   They held their staves between the two men, and the herald Idaios
IL.7.278   κῆρυξ Ἰδαῖος πεπνυμένα μήδεα εἰδώς:

IL.7.278  out of his knowledge of prudent advices spoke a word to them:
IL.7.279  μηκέτι παῖδε φίλω πολεμίζετε μηδὲ μάχεσθον:
IL.7.279  'Stop the fight, dear children, nor go on with this battle.
IL.7.280  ἀμφοτέρω γὰρ σφῶϊ φιλεῖ νεφεληγερέτα Ζεύς,
IL.7.280  To Zeus who gathers the clouds both of you are beloved,
IL.7.281  ἄμφω δ' αἰχμητά: τό γε δὴ καὶ ἴδμεν ἅπαντες.
IL.7.281  and both of you are fighters; this thing all of us know surely.
IL.7.282  νὺξ δ' ἤδη τελέθει: ἀγαθὸν καὶ νυκτὶ πιθέσθαι.
IL.7.282  Night darkens now. It is a good thing to give way to the night-time.'

The phrase καί νύ κε δὴ ξιφέεσσ' αὐτοσχεδὸν οὐτάζοντο (273) is used only here in the *Iliad*, although a similar line is used in Book 17 to describe a battle between Hector and Automedon:

IL.17.530  καί νύ κε δὴ ξιφέεσσ' αὐτοσχεδὸν ὡρμηθήτην
IL.17.530  And now they would have gone for each other with swords at close quarters,

In this case, however, the progression from spear shot range

IL.17.525  Ἕκτωρ δ' Αὐτομέδοντος ἀκόντισε δουρὶ φαεινῷ:
IL.17.525  Then Hektor made a cast with the shining spear at Automedon,
IL.17.526  ἀλλ' ὃ μὲν ἄντα ἰδὼν ἠλεύατο χάλκεον ἔγχος:
IL.17.526  but he, keeping his eyes straight on him, avoided the bronze spear.

to a contrafactual expression of sword stab range

IL.17.530  καί νύ κε δὴ ξιφέεσσ' αὐτοσχεδὸν ὡρμηθήτην
IL.17.530  And now they would have gone for each other with swords at close quarters,
IL.17.531  εἰ μή σφω' Αἴαντε διέκριναν μεμαῶτε,
IL.17.531  had not the two Aiantes driven strongly between them,

occurs logically and without the need for *ad hoc* correction, as though Homer learned his lesson in Book 7. Thus, in lines 264-73, Homer takes advantage of the flexibility of his verbal medium by reversing a previous spatial configuration to serve a present dramatic purpose.[163]

---

[163] Cf. Andersen (1990: *passim*), Jones (1992), and Braswell (1971: *passim*) for a similar *ad hoc* manipulation of time in the *Iliad*, time in the *Odyssey*, and mythological paradigms in the *Iliad*, respectively.

Mortals are not, however, the only characters whose actions are represented through intercutting. Two times in the *Iliad* the Olympian gods alternate between Greek and Trojan lines of battle to mirror a similar development occurring between the human characters. In Book 17 the Greeks and Trojans fight over Patroclus' corpse. Up to this point, the action has constantly shifted from side to side.[164] In line 543, an establishing shot imposes a temporary pause in the action:

IL.17.543  ἂψ δ' ἐπὶ Πατρόκλῳ τέτατο κρατερὴ ὑσμίνη
IL.17.543  Once again over Patroklos was close drawn a strong battle
IL.17.544  ἀργαλέη πολύδακρυς, ἔγειρε δὲ νεῖκος Ἀθήνη
IL.17.544  weary and sorrowful, and Athene from the sky descending

Then, rather than return immediately to one side or the other, Homer intercuts between Athena and Apollo as they occupy the Greek and Trojan lines, respectively. First he has Athena disguise herself as Phoinix, descend from Olympus to the Greek line of battle, and encourage Menelaos to persuade the Greeks to continue to protect Patroclus' corpse (544-59). Menelaos assures Athena that all he needs in order to carry out her wishes is divine strength. She provides it to him and he displays his new-found strength by killing a Trojan warrior (560-81). Then Apollo disguises himself as Phainops, encounters Hector on the Trojan line of battle, and fuels his desire to attack Menelaos (17.582-90). It is in lines 593-96, however, that the parallel nature of mortal and immortal intercutting becomes most conspicuous, when Zeus flashes his thunderbolt,

IL.17.593  καὶ τότ' ἄρα Κρονίδης ἕλετ' αἰγίδα θυσσανόεσσαν
IL.17.593  And now the son of Kronos caught up the betasselled
IL.17.594  μαρμαρέην, Ἴδην δὲ κατὰ νεφέεσσι κάλυψεν,
IL.17.594  glaring aegis, and shrouded Ida in mists. He let go
IL.17.595  ἀστράψας δὲ μάλα μεγάλ' ἔκτυπε, τὴν δ' ἐτίναξε,
IL.17.595  a lightning flash and a loud thunderstroke, shaking the mountain,
IL.17.596  νίκην δὲ Τρώεσσι δίδου, ἐφόβησε δ' Ἀχαιούς.
IL.17.596  gave victory to the Trojans, and terrified the Achaians.

---

[164] E.g., 17.394.

reminiscent of the clash between mortals on the battlefield that often concludes an intercutting series.

In a more elaborate version of the previous scene, the divine allies of each army gather on the Greek and Trojan lines of battle:

IL.20.32    βὰν δ' ἴμεναι πόλεμόνδε θεοὶ δίχα θυμὸν ἔχοντες:
IL.20.32    and the gods went down to enter the fighting, with purposes opposed.
IL.20.33    Ἥρη μὲν μετ' ἀγῶνα νεῶν καὶ Παλλὰς Ἀθήνη
IL.20.33    Hera went to the assembled ships with Pallas Athene
IL.20.34    ἠδὲ Ποσειδάων γαιήοχος ἠδ' ἐριούνης
IL.20.34    and with Poseidon who embraces the earth, and with generous
IL.20.35    Ἑρμείας, ὃς ἐπὶ φρεσὶ πευκαλίμῃσι κέκασται:
IL.20.35    Hermes, who within the heart is armed with astute thoughts.
IL.20.36    Ἥφαιστος δ' ἅμα τοῖσι κίε σθένεϊ βλεμεαίνων
IL.20.36    Hephaistos went the way of these in the pride of his great strength
IL.20.37    χωλεύων, ὑπὸ δὲ κνῆμαι ῥώοντο ἀραιαί.
IL.20.37    limping, and yet his shrunken legs moved lightly beneath him.
IL.20.38    ἐς δὲ Τρῶας Ἄρης κορυθαίολος, αὐτὰρ ἅμ' αὐτῷ
IL.20.38    But Ares of the shining helm went over to the Trojans,
IL.20.39    Φοῖβος ἀκερσεκόμης ἠδ' Ἄρτεμις ἰοχέαιρα
IL.20.39    and with him Phoibos of the unshorn hair, and the lady of arrows
IL.20.40    Λητώ τε Ξάνθός τε φιλομμειδής τ' Ἀφροδίτη.
IL.20.40    Artemis, and smiling Aphrodite, Leto, and Xanthos.

Both Athena and Ares deliver a war cry in their respective terrestrial locations:

IL.20.48    αὖε δ' Ἀθήνη
IL.20.48    and Athene bellowed
IL.20.49    στᾶσ' ὁτὲ μὲν παρὰ τάφρον ὀρυκτὴν τείχεος ἐκτός,
IL.20.49    standing now beside the ditch dug at the wall's outside
IL.20.50    ἄλλοτ' ἐπ' ἀκτάων ἐριδούπων μακρὸν ἀΰτει.
IL.20.50    and now again at the thundering sea's edge gave out her great cry,
IL.20.51    αὖε δ' Ἄρης ἑτέρωθεν ἐρεμνῇ λαίλαπι ἶσος
IL.20.51    while on the other side Ares in the likeness of a dark stormcloud
IL.20.52    ὀξὺ κατ' ἀκροτάτης πόλιος Τρώεσσι κελεύων,
IL.20.52    bellowed, now from the peak of the citadel urging the Trojans

Then Zeus, Poseidon, and Hades reciprocate, symbolizing the comprehensive scope of the impending battle in all four corners of the universe:

79

IL.20.56  δεινὸν δ' ἐβρόντησε πατὴρ ἀνδρῶν τε θεῶν τε

IL.20.56  From high above the father of gods and men made thunder

IL.20.57  ὑψόθεν: αὐτὰρ ἔνερθε Ποσειδάων ἐτίναξε

IL.20.57  terribly, while Poseidon from deep under them shuddered

IL.20.58  γαῖαν ἀπειρεσίην ὀρέων τ' αἰπεινὰ κάρηνα.

IL.20.58  all the illimitable earth, the sheer heads of the mountains.

IL.20.59  πάντες δ' ἐσσείοντο πόδες πολυπίδακος Ἴδης

IL.20.59  And all the feet of Ida with her many waters were shaken

IL.20.60  καὶ κορυφαί, Τρώων τε πόλις καὶ νῆες Ἀχαιῶν.

IL.20.60  and all her crests, and the city of Troy, the ships of the Achaians.

IL.20.61  ἔδδεισεν δ' ὑπένερθεν ἄναξ ἐνέρων Ἀϊδωνεύς,

IL.20.61  Aïdoneus, lord of the dead below, was in terror

IL.20.62  δείσας δ' ἐκ θρόνου ἆλτο καὶ ἴαχε, μή οἱ ὕπερθε

IL.20.62  and sprang from his throne and screamed aloud, for fear that above him

Then in lines 66-74 we realize that the gods are not merely intervening in human affairs, as Zeus' *laissez-faire* attitude in lines 24-5 encourages,[165] but actually engaging in warfare against *each other*:

IL.20.66  τόσσος ἄρα κτύπος ὦρτο θεῶν ἔριδι ξυνιόντων.

IL.20.66  such was the crash that sounded as the gods came driving together

IL.20.67  ἤτοι μὲν γὰρ ἔναντα Ποσειδάωνος ἄνακτος

IL.20.67  in wrath. For now over against the lord Poseidon

IL.20.68  ἵστατ' Ἀπόλλων Φοῖβος ἔχων ἰὰ πτερόεντα,

IL.20.68  Phoibos Apollo took his stand with his feathered arrows,

IL.20.69  ἄντα δ' Ἐνυαλίοιο θεὰ γλαυκῶπις Ἀθήνη:

IL.20.69  and against Enyalios the goddess grey-eyed Athene.

IL.20.70  Ἥρῃ δ' ἀντέστη χρυσηλάκατος κελαδεινὴ

IL.20.70  Against Hera stood the lady of clamour, of the golden distaff,

IL.20.71  Ἄρτεμις ἰοχέαιρα κασιγνήτη ἑκάτοιο:

IL.20.71  of the showering arrows, Artemis, sister of the far striker.

IL.20.72  Λητοῖ δ' ἀντέστη σῶκος ἐριούνιος Ἑρμῆς,

IL.20.72  Opposite Leto stood the strong one, generous Hermes,

IL.20.73  ἄντα δ' ἄρ' Ἡφαίστοιο μέγας ποταμὸς βαθυδίνης,

IL.20.73  and against Hephaistos stood the great deep-eddying river

IL.20.74  ὃν Ξάνθον καλέουσι θεοί, ἄνδρες δὲ Σκάμανδρον.

IL.20.74  who is called Xanthos by the gods, but by mortals Skamandros.

Thus, the intercutting in this scene does not merely reflect human intercutting, as in the battle over Patroclus' corpse, but constitutes a first-

---

[165] Cf. *Il.* 20.24-5.

order implementation of the device in its own right, linking mortal and immortal movement within Iliadic story space. In the next two chapters we encounter yet another way in which Homer links mortal and immortal characters: through their shared *perception*, of both visible and imaginary spaces.

# META-AUDIENCE

"Experienced as it is by the human characters...and, at the same time, looked upon by the gods, the action of the [Homeric] poems is scrutinized in its depths. Light is projected upon it from many angles." (Vivante, 1970: 32)

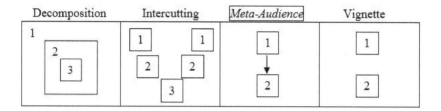

Meta-audience consists of characters watching other characters.[166] Homer establishes four main locations within the *Iliad*—two aerial, two terrestrial—as permanent spectatorial venues. The aerial meta-theaters consist of Olympus, abode of the gods, and Mount Ida, to which the gods frequently descend for an intimate view of the mortal action. The Olympian gods peruse the Trojan plain so often, in fact, that Michael Silk considers their reactions to human events to be their sole narrative function.[167] Indeed, in one scene the narrator emphasizes the absence of all except one minor deity to witness the battle between Greeks and Trojans from Olympus, as though to imply that they are otherwise always present:

IL.11.74 οἴη γάρ ῥα θεῶν παρετύγχανε μαρναμένοισιν,
IL.11.74 She alone of all the immortals attended this action
IL.11.75 οἳ δ' ἄλλοι οὔ σφιν πάρεσαν θεοί, ἀλλὰ ἕκηλοι
IL.11.75 but the other immortals were not there, but sat quietly
IL.11.76 σφοῖσιν ἐνὶ μεγάροισι καθείατο, ἧχι ἑκάστῳ
IL.11.76 remote and apart in their palaces, where for each one of them
IL.11.77 δώματα καλὰ τέτυκτο κατὰ πτύχας Οὐλύμποιο.
IL.11.77 a house had been built in splendour along the folds of Olympos.

---

[166] Cf. Edwards (1987: 84); Edmunds (1996: 3).
[167] 1987: 80.

Despite their frequent focus on mortal activity, however, the attention of the gods is by no means monopolized by it. Occasionally they even watch *each other*, as when Hera directs her gaze at Poseidon and Zeus on two separate stages:

IL.14.153  Ἥρη δ' εἰσεῖδε χρυσόθρονος ὀφθαλμοῖσι
IL.14.153  Now Hera, she of the golden throne, standing on Olympos'
IL.14.154  στᾶσ' ἐξ Οὐλύμποιο ἀπὸ ῥίου: αὐτίκα δ' ἔγνω
IL.14.154  horn, looked out with her eyes, and saw at once how Poseidon,
IL.14.155  τὸν μὲν ποιπνύοντα μάχην ἀνὰ κυδιάνειραν
IL.14.155  who was her very brother and her lord's brother, was bustling
IL.14.156  αὐτοκασίγνητον καὶ δαέρα, χαῖρε δὲ θυμῷ:
IL.14.156  about the battle where men win glory, and her heart was happy.
IL.14.157  Ζῆνα δ' ἐπ' ἀκροτάτης κορυφῆς πολυπίδακος Ἴδης
IL.14.157  Then she saw Zeus, sitting along the loftiest summit
IL.14.158  ἥμενον εἰσεῖδε, στυγερὸς δέ οἱ ἔπλετο θυμῷ.
IL.14.158  on Ida of the springs, and in her eyes he was hateful.

The gods also play a crucial dramatic role in their own right.[168] Frequently they act on their own volition, even take part in the fighting themselves, as when Zeus watches a battle between several Olympians in Book 21:

IL.21.385  ἐν δ' ἄλλοισι θεοῖσιν ἔρις πέσε βεβριθυῖα
IL.21.385  But upon the other gods descended the wearisome burden
IL.21.386  ἀργαλέη, δίχα δέ σφιν ἐνὶ φρεσὶ θυμὸς ἄητο:
IL.21.386  of hatred, and the wind of their fury blew from division,
IL.21.387  σὺν δ' ἔπεσον μεγάλῳ πατάγῳ, βράχε δ' εὐρεῖα χθών,
IL.21.387  and they collided with a grand crash, the broad earth echoing
IL.21.388  ἀμφὶ δὲ σάλπιγξεν μέγας οὐρανός. ἄϊε δὲ Ζεὺς
IL.21.388  and the huge sky sounded as with trumpets. Zeus heard it
IL.21.389  ἥμενος Οὐλύμπῳ: ἐγέλασσε δέ οἱ φίλον ἦτορ
IL.21.389  from where he sat on Olympos, and was amused in his deep heart
IL.21.390  γηθοσύνῃ, ὅθ' ὁρᾶτο θεοὺς ἔριδι ξυνιόντας.
IL.21.390  for pleasure, as he watched the gods' collision in conflict.

The most common activity of the gods, however, is to watch the mortal drama and to descend either to Ida or the Trojan plain or to ascend to

---

[168] Cf. Redfield (1975: 229).

Olympus *from* the Trojan plain. Excursions to and from Olympus are frequent and often elaborately described.[169] On the other hand, sometimes the action shifts there without prior notice and takes the audience by surprise, as in the following scenario described by Richardson:

> When Achilles is chasing Hector around the citadel before the inevitable duel, we are joined as spectators not only by the Greek army and the Trojan populace, but also by the gods...(*Il.* 22.165-70)...We suddenly find ourselves on Olympus, though after a fashion we have been viewing the chase from there as long as the gods have.[170]

This technique is especially effective when the transition occurs in mid-verse rather than in initial or final position, accentuating its unexpected quality, as in the sudden cut from the Trojan plain to Olympus in line 4 of Book 15:

IL.15.1 αὐτὰρ ἐπεὶ διά τε σκόλοπας καὶ τάφρον ἔβησαν
IL.15.1 But after they had crossed back over the ditch and the sharp stakes
IL.15.2 φεύγοντες, πολλοὶ δὲ δάμεν Δαναῶν ὑπὸ χερσίν,
IL.15.2 in flight, and many had gone down under the hands of the Danaans,
IL.15.3 οἳ μὲν δὴ παρ' ὄχεσφιν ἐρητύοντο μένοντες
IL.15.3 they checked about once more and stood their ground by the chariots,
IL.15.4 χλωροὶ ὑπαὶ δείους πεφοβημένοι· ἔγρετο δὲ Ζεὺς
IL.15.4 green for fear and terrified. But now Zeus wakened
IL.15.5 Ἴδης ἐν κορυφῇσι παρὰ χρυσοθρόνου Ἥρης,
IL.15.5 by Hera of the gold throne on the high places of Ida,
IL.15.6 στῆ δ' ἄρ' ἀναΐξας, ἴδε δὲ Τρῶας καὶ Ἀχαιοὺς
IL.15.6 and stood suddenly upright, and saw the Achaians and Trojans,
IL.15.7 τοὺς μὲν ὀρινομένους, τοὺς δὲ κλονέοντας ὄπισθεν
IL.15.7 these driven to flight, the others harrying them in confusion,
IL.15.8 Ἀργείους, μετὰ δέ σφι Ποσειδάωνα ἄνακτα·
IL.15.8 these last Argives, and saw among them the lord Poseidon.

Sudden shifts to a given meta-theater often bring us back quickly to the point of origin, as when Zeus considers a course of revenge for the death of Sarpedon:

---

[169] Cf. Chapter 2, above.
[170] 1990: 112.

IL.16.644  ὡς ἄρα τοὶ περὶ νεκρὸν ὁμίλεον, οὐδέ ποτε Ζεὺς
IL.16.644  So they swarmed over the dead man, nor did Zeus ever
IL.16.645  τρέψεν ἀπὸ κρατερῆς ὑσμίνης ὄσσε φαεινώ,
IL.16.645  turn the glaring of his eyes from the strong encounter,
IL.16.646  ἀλλὰ κατ' αὐτοὺς αἰὲν ὅρα καὶ φράζετο θυμῷ,
IL.16.646  but kept gazing forever upon them, in spirit reflective,
IL.16.647  πολλὰ μάλ' ἀμφὶ φόνῳ Πατρόκλου μερμηρίζων,
IL.16.647  and pondered hard over many ways for the death of Patroclus;

After this brief meditation in Olympus the action returns to the Trojan plain, where Zeus' plan to avenge his son begins to materialize. Sometimes, however, the action lingers in the new location and initiates a scene between two or more Olympians, as when Zeus addresses Athena following what seems to be a routine jaunt to Olympus:

IL.19.338  ὡς ἔφατο κλαίων, ἐπὶ δὲ στενάχοντο γέροντες,
IL.19.338  So he spoke, mourning, and the elders lamented around him
IL.19.339  μνησάμενοι τὰ ἕκαστος ἐνὶ μεγάροισιν ἔλειπε:
IL.19.339  remembering each those he had left behind in his own halls.
IL.19.340  μυρομένους δ' ἄρα τούς γε ἰδὼν ἐλέησε Κρονίων,
IL.19.340  The son of Kronos took pity on them as he watched them mourning
IL.19.341  αἶψα δ' Ἀθηναίην ἔπεα πτερόεντα προσηύδα:
IL.19.341  and immediately spoke in winged words to Athene:

In either case, these frequent excursions to Olympus accentuate its offstage status, inducing the impression that at any moment we might be transported there, its divine inhabitants waiting in the wings, akin to what cinematographer Bill Butler achieves in the movie "Jaws":[171]

We kept the camera at water-level whenever we could. And it isn't something that you will see immediately, but after awhile you begin to feel that that shark was maybe just under that water. And by keeping the camera down close to that water, we built into the picture a kind of atmosphere or feeling that we wouldn't have gotten any other way.

This technique applies as well to Ida, as when Zeus wakes up after Hera seduces him in 15.1-8, as well as between Ida and Olympus, as when Zeus catches Hera and Athena preparing to descend to the Trojan plain to

---

[171] 2000.

help the Greeks in 8.397. Olympus and Ida, however, are not the only permanent meta-theaters in the *Iliad* (not the only sharks in the sea, so to speak), and the action does not shift to these locations frequently enough to generate such anticipatory anxiety automatically. Therefore, as a subtle reminder of their imminent presence, characters frequently refer to the gods in their capacity as meta-spectators:

IL.2.26    νῦν δ' ἐμέθεν ξύνες ὦκα: Διὸς δέ τοι ἄγγελός εἰμι,
IL.2.26    Listen quickly to what I say, since I am a messenger
IL.2.27    ὅς σεῦ ἄνευθεν ἐὼν μέγα κήδεται ἠδ' ἐλεαίρει.
IL.2.27    of Zeus, who far away cares much for you and is pitiful.

or the narrator reports that a character's prayer is acknowledged

IL.1.43    ὣς ἔφατ' εὐχόμενος, τοῦ δ' ἔκλυε Φοῖβος Ἀπόλλων,
IL.1.43    So he spoke in prayer, and Phoibos Apollo heard him,

or disregarded

IL.2.419    ὣς ἔφατ', οὐδ' ἄρα πώ οἱ ἐπεκραίαινε Κρονίων,
IL.2.419    He spoke, but none of this would the son of Kronos accomplish,

by a given deity, thereby evoking Olympus without a full-scale change of scene.

Although not alone in the role of meta-spectator, Zeus determines the meta-theatrical agenda of the *Iliad* more than any other deity.[172] In the following analysis of Books 8 and 9—where his influence, and that of Olympus, is both most and least felt, respectively—we see how his absence or presence can influence the nature and course of the mortal action. We begin in Olympus, at the beginning of Book 8. Zeus convokes a meeting with the other deities (8.1-4). He instructs them to stay out of the war, and travels to Ida to assume his usual function as meta-spectator:

---

[172] Cf. Silk (1987: 80).

IL.8.47 Ἴδην δ' ἵκανεν πολυπίδακα μητέρα θηρῶν
IL.8.47 He came to Ida with all her springs, the mother of wild beasts,
IL.8.48 Γάργαρον, ἔνθά δέ οἱ τέμενος βωμός τε θυήεις.
IL.8.48 to Gargaron, where was his holy ground and his smoking altar.
IL.8.49 ἔνθ' ἵππους ἔστησε πατὴρ ἀνδρῶν τε θεῶν τε
IL.8.49 There the father of gods and of mortals halted his horses,
IL.8.50 λύσας ἐξ ὀχέων, κατὰ δ' ἠέρα πουλὺν ἔχευεν.
IL.8.50 and slipped them from their harness, and drifted close mist about them,
IL.8.51 αὐτὸς δ' ἐν κορυφῇσι καθέζετο κύδεϊ γαίων
IL.8.51 and himself rejoicing in the pride of his strength sat down on the mountain
IL.8.52 εἰσορόων Τρώων τε πόλιν καὶ νῆας Ἀχαιῶν.
IL.8.52 looking out over the city of Troy and the ships of the Achaians.

The *dramatis personae* enter the Trojan plain, beginning with the Greeks at stage-left:

IL.8.53 οἳ δ' ἄρα δεῖπνον ἕλοντο κάρη κομόωντες Ἀχαιοὶ
IL.8.53 Now the flowing-haired Achaians had taken their dinner
IL.8.54 ῥίμφα κατὰ κλισίας, ἀπὸ δ' αὐτοῦ θωρήσσοντο.
IL.8.54 lightly among their shelters, and they put on their armour thereafter;

and the Trojans at stage right:

IL.8.55 Τρῶες δ' αὖθ' ἑτέρωθεν ἀνὰ πτόλιν ὡπλίζοντο
IL.8.55 and on the other side, in the city, the Trojans took up
IL.8.56 παυρότεροι: μέμασαν δὲ καὶ ὡς ὑσμῖνι μάχεσθαι
IL.8.56 their armour, fewer men, yet minded to stand the encounter
IL.8.57 χρειοῖ ἀναγκαίῃ, πρό τε παίδων καὶ πρὸ γυναικῶν.
IL.8.57 even so, caught in necessity, for their wives and their children.
IL.8.58 πᾶσαι δ' ὠΐγνυντο πύλαι, ἐκ δ' ἔσσυτο λαός,
IL.8.58 And all the gates were made open, and the fighting men swept through them,
IL.8.59 πεζοί θ' ἱππῆές τε: πολὺς δ' ὀρυμαγδὸς ὀρώρει.
IL.8.59 the foot ranks and the horsemen, and the sound grew huge of their onset.

Finally, both Greeks and Trojans converge onto center stage:

IL.8.60 οἳ δ' ὅτε δή ῥ' ἐς χῶρον ἕνα ξυνιόντες ἵκοντο
IL.8.60 Now as these advancing came to one place and encountered,
IL.8.61 σύν ῥ' ἔβαλον ῥινούς, σὺν δ' ἔγχεα καὶ μένε' ἀνδρῶν
IL.8.61 they dashed their shields together and their spears, and the strength of
IL.8.62 χαλκεοθωρήκων: ἀτὰρ ἀσπίδες ὀμφαλόεσσαι
IL.8.62 armoured men in bronze, and the shields massive in the middle
IL.8.63 ἔπληντ' ἀλλήλῃσι, πολὺς δ' ὀρυμαγδὸς ὀρώρει.
IL.8.63 clashed against each other, and the sound grew huge of the fighting.

IL.8.64 ἔνθα δ' ἄμ' οἰμωγή τε καὶ εὐχωλὴ πέλεν ἀνδρῶν
IL.8.64 There the screaming and the shouts of triumph rose up together
IL.8.65 ὀλλύντων τε καὶ ὀλλυμένων, ῥέε δ' αἵματι γαῖα.
IL.8.65 of men killing and men killed, and the ground ran blood.

Rather than delve into the meta-performance proper, however, the scene shifts immediately back to Ida, where Zeus, upon determining that the Trojans will get the better of the Greeks, flashes his thunderbolt above the mortal stage, providing a first-order spectacle for the Greeks and a third-order spectacle for the audience through the eyes of the Greeks as seen through the eyes of Zeus:

IL.8.75 αὐτὸς δ' ἐξ Ἴδης μεγάλ' ἔκτυπε, δαιόμενον δὲ
IL.8.75 and he himself crashed a great stroke from Ida, and a kindling
IL.8.76 ἧκε σέλας μετὰ λαὸν Ἀχαιῶν: οἳ δὲ ἰδόντες
IL.8.76 flash shot over the people of the Achaians; seeing it
IL.8.77 θάμβησαν, καὶ πάντας ὑπὸ χλωρὸν δέος εἷλεν.
IL.8.77 they were stunned, and pale terror took hold of all of them.

Thus, both the Greeks, on the one hand, and Zeus, on the other, become meta-spectacle and meta-spectator simultaneously.[173] Then the mortal spectacle resumes, until the Greeks threaten to bypass Zeus' pro-Trojan agenda, resulting in another shift to Ida, where Zeus looks down onto the battlefield and again flashes his thunderbolt. This time his appearance is more explicitly acknowledged by the Greeks, in Nestor's address to Diomedes:

IL.8.139 Τυδεΐδη ἄγε δ' αὖτε φόβονδ' ἔχε μώνυχας ἵππους.
IL.8.139 'Son of Tydeus, steer now to flight your single-foot horses.
IL.8.140 ἦ οὐ γινώσκεις ὅ τοι ἐκ Διὸς οὐχ ἔπετ' ἀλκή;
IL.8.140 Can you not see that the power of Zeus no longer is with you?

Yet the scene shifts again to the Trojan plain, where Hector acknowledges Zeus' favoritism and encourages the Trojans to take advantage of it. We expect a return to Ida, in conformity to the pattern that seems to be emerging in Book 8. Yet after Hector's boastful speech

---

[173] Cf. Wood (1987: 28, 38).

in lines 173-83, the action shifts, not to Zeus on Ida, but rather to Hera on Olympus:

IL.8.198  ὣς ἔφατ' εὐχόμενος, νεμέσησε δὲ πότνια Ἥρη,
IL.8.198  So he spoke, boasting, and the lady Hera was angry,
IL.8.199  σείσατο δ' εἰνὶ θρόνῳ, ἐλέλιξε δὲ μακρὸν Ὄλυμπον,
IL.8.199  and started upon her throne, and tall Olympos was shaken,

Thus, three concurrent meta-theaters are established: Olympus and Ida with their view of the Trojan plain, and the Trojan plain with its view of Zeus' pyrotechnics, *sema* of divine intervention.[174] What begins as a simple meta-theater in line 52 expands into a three-tier dramatic complex, facilitating immortal spectatorship from and travel between Olympus and Ida, while the mortal action transpires upon the Trojan plain along the horizontal continuum between the Greek camp and Troy. Such spatial polyphony displays a resourcefulness denied even to film, whose horizontal viewing area precludes symmetrical correspondence between its x and y axes. That is not to say, however, that this handicap is inherent to the filmic medium. On the contrary, Eisenstein insists that if the horizontal movie-screen were to be replaced by a square one, cinema could conceivably do justice to the complementary forces of horizontal and vertical action:[175]

...for thirty years we have been content to see excluded 50 per cent of composition possibilities, in consequence of the *horizontal shape* of the frame. By the word "excluded" I refer to all the possibilities of *vertical, upright composition*....that loathsome upper part of the frame...has bent and bound us to a passive horizontalism...

This is, in fact, precisely the balance achieved by Homer. Rather than focus primarily upon horizontal action, as in the *Odyssey*, the constant presence of Zeus as meta-spectator and of Olympus and Ida as meta-theaters enriches the spatial dimension of the *Iliad* and prevents receptive

---

[174] While acknowledging that "such omnipresence" is denied to theater, Münsterberg (1970: 44) considers it to be an exclusively cinematic technique.

[175] 1970a: 49. Cf. Stansbury-O'Donnell (1999: 156).

complacency. At any given point the action might shift left, right, above, or below, each location within eyeshot of the others, susceptible to abrupt or gradual transitions between them. In line 350 of Book 8, for example, after 138 lines of battle that result in a Greek rout, Hera and Athena decide to descend to the Trojan plain and to help the Greeks, despite Zeus' prohibition against divine intervention at the beginning of the book. This initiates a meta-narrative between Zeus, Hera, and Athena that transpires on the vertical dimension of story space in counterpoint to the main action on the Trojan plain. As the goddesses descend from Olympus, the scene shifts to Ida through the meta-spectatorship of Zeus,

IL.8.396   τῇ ῥα δι' αὐτάων κεντρηνεκέας ἔχον ἵππους.
IL.8.396   Through the way between they held the speed of their goaded horses.
IL.8.397   Ζεὺς δὲ πατὴρ Ἴδηθεν ἐπεὶ ἴδε χώσατ' ἄρ' αἰνῶς,
IL.8.397   But Zeus father, watching from Ida, was angered terribly

who sends Iris to Olympus to prevent them from continuing their journey:

IL.8.409   ὣς ἔφατ', ὦρτο δὲ Ἶρις ἀελλόπος ἀγγελέουσα,
IL.8.409   He spoke, and Iris, storm-footed, rose with his message
IL.8.410   βῆ δὲ κατ' Ἰδαίων ὀρέων ἐς μακρὸν Ὄλυμπον.
IL.8.410   and took her way from the peaks of Ida to tall Olympos,
IL.8.411   πρώτῃσιν δὲ πύλῃσι πολυπτύχου Οὐλύμποιο
IL.8.411   and at the utmost gates of many-folded Olympos
IL.8.412   ἀντομένη κατέρυκε, Διὸς δέ σφ' ἔννεπε μῦθον:
IL.8.412   met and stayed them, and spoke the word that Zeus had given her:

Hera and Athena obey Zeus' orders and he returns to Olympus, where he threatens them and warns them to honor his authority. Hera feebly objects, resulting in an even greater expression of Zeus' absolute power. The scene ends with Hera's pregnant silence and the conclusion of this divine meta-narrative through ring composition, a curtain-call of Greek and Trojan *dramatis personae* arranged symmetrically upon the Trojan stage:

IL.8.484   ὣς φάτο, τὸν δ' οὔ τι προσέφη λευκώλενος Ἥρη.

IL.8.484  So he spoke, and Hera of the white arms gave him no answer.
IL.8.485  ἐν δ' ἔπεσ' Ὠκεανῷ λαμπρὸν φάος ἠελίοιο
IL.8.485  And now the shining light of the sun was dipped in the Ocean
IL.8.486  ἕλκον νύκτα μέλαιναν ἐπὶ ζείδωρον ἄρουραν.
IL.8.486  trailing black night across the grain-giving land. For the Trojans
IL.8.487  Τρωσὶν μέν ῥ' ἀέκουσιν ἔδυ φάος, αὐτὰρ Ἀχαιοῖς
IL.8.487  the daylight sank against their will, but for the Achaians
IL.8.488  ἀσπασίη τρίλλιστος ἐπήλυθε νὺξ ἐρεβεννή.
IL.8.488  sweet and thrice-supplicated was the coming on of the dark night.

Homer, then, uses meta-audience to frame lines 1-488 of Book 8, encompassing the action within two Olympian episodes. Once, however, the Trojans assemble near the Greek ships and Hector delivers a speech urging them to cease fighting until the next day and to pay tribute to the gods, the atmosphere grows ominous, lacking the sense of divine presence permeating the previous scenes, as though the Olympians have left the stage:

IL.8.548  ἔρδον δ' ἀθανάτοισι τεληέσσας ἑκατόμβας
IL.8.548  They accomplished likewise full sacrifices before the immortals,
IL.8.549  κνίσην δ' ἐκ πεδίου ἄνεμοι φέρον οὐρανὸν εἴσω.
IL.8.549  and the winds wafted the savour aloft from the plain to the heavens
IL.8.550  ἡδεῖαν: τῆς δ' οὔ τι θεοὶ μάκαρες δατέοντο,
IL.8.550  in its fragrance; and yet the blessed gods took no part of it.
IL.8.551  οὐδ' ἔθελον: μάλα γάρ σφιν ἀπήχθετο Ἴλιος ἱρή
IL.8.551  They would not; so hateful to them was sacred Ilion,
IL.8.552  καὶ Πρίαμος καὶ λαὸς ἐϋμμελίω Πριάμοιο
IL.8.552  and Priam, and the city of Priam of the strong ash spear.

In his speech to the Greeks at the beginning of Book 9, Agamemnon chastizes Zeus as though he is no longer within earshot:

IL.9.17  ὦ φίλοι Ἀργείων ἡγήτορες ἠδὲ μέδοντες
IL.9.17  'Friends, who are leaders of the Argives and keep their counsel:
IL.9.18  Ζεύς με μέγα Κρονίδης ἄτῃ ἐνέδησε βαρείῃ
IL.9.18  Zeus son of Kronos has caught me badly in bitter futility.
IL.9.19  σχέτλιος, ὃς πρὶν μέν μοι ὑπέσχετο καὶ κατένευσεν
IL.9.19  He is hard: who before this time promised me and consented
IL.9.20  Ἴλιον ἐκπέρσαντ' εὐτείχεον ἀπονέεσθαι,
IL.9.20  that I might sack strong-walled Ilion and sail homeward.

IL.9.21   νῦν δὲ κακὴν ἀπάτην βουλεύσατο, καί με κελεύει
IL.9.21   Now he has devised a vile deception and bids me go back
IL.9.22   δυσκλέα Ἄργος ἱκέσθαι, ἐπεὶ πολὺν ὤλεσα λαόν.
IL.9.22   to Argos in dishonour having lost many of my people.

Diomedes and Nestor urge the Greeks to stay the course rather than to desert the war as Agamemnon advises, and Nestor urges Agamemnon to petition Achilles to reenter the fray, evoking Zeus in a reverential light:

IL.9.96   Ἀτρεΐδη κύδιστε ἄναξ ἀνδρῶν Ἀγάμεμνον
IL.9.96   'Son of Atreus, most lordly and king of men, Agamemnon,
IL.9.97   ἐν σοὶ μὲν λήξω, σέο δ' ἄρξομαι, οὕνεκα πολλῶν
IL.9.97   with you I will end, with you I will make my beginning, since you
IL.9.98   λαῶν ἔσσι ἄναξ καί τοι Ζεὺς ἐγγυάλιξε
IL.9.98   are lord over many people, and Zeus has given into your hand
IL.9.99   σκῆπτρόν τ' ἠδὲ θέμιστας, ἵνά σφισι βουλεύησθα.
IL.9.99   the sceptre and rights of judgment, to be king over the people.

Agamemnon reiterates Nestor's sentiment, evoking Zeus with a similar degree of subtlety:

IL.9.116   ἀασάμην, οὐδ' αὐτὸς ἀναίνομαι. ἀντί νυ πολλῶν
IL.9.116   I was mad, I myself will not deny it. Worth many
IL.9.117   λαῶν ἐστὶν ἀνὴρ ὅν τε Ζεὺς κῆρι φιλήσῃ,
IL.9.117   fighters is that man whom Zeus in his heart loves, as now
IL.9.118   ὡς νῦν τοῦτον ἔτισε, δάμασσε δὲ λαὸν Ἀχαιῶν.
IL.9.118   he has honoured this man and beaten down the Achaian people.

This sets the stage for a reappearance of Zeus, to sanction the present turn of events and to reaffirm his essential function as dramatic chaperon. To initiate this reaffirmation of divine guidance, Nestor concludes his elaborate plans for an embassy to Achilles with the intention to win Zeus' support:

IL.9.171   φέρτε δὲ χερσὶν ὕδωρ, εὐφημῆσαί τε κέλεσθε,
IL.9.171   Bring also water for their hands, and bid them keep words of good omen,
IL.9.172   ὄφρα Διὶ Κρονίδῃ ἀρησόμεθ', αἴ κ' ἐλεήσῃ.
IL.9.172   so we may pray to Zeus, son of Kronos, if he will have pity.'

In lines 174-76, the Greeks pour a libation to Zeus, leading us to expect either a favorable or unfavorable response from him. He completely ignores it, however. In lines 182-84, the Greeks pray to Poseidon for help in their mission as they travel along the shore to Achilles' shelter. He ignores their plea as well. Thus, despite the wealth of supplicatory activity from the beginning of Book 9, the Olympians remain offstage and the terrestrial action transpires within the same dramatic vacuum initiated at the end of Book 8. Indeed, when the Greeks finally encounter Achilles, his subsequent refusal of their offer merely confirms their spiritual alienation, contrasting markedly with the numinosity of the previous book.

In addition to the gods, mortals also frequently serve as meta-spectators in the *Iliad*. They focalize, for instance, emotions such as amazement,[176] joy,[177] courage,[178] and fear.[179] Sometimes, on the other hand, two characters or groups of characters react differently to a given meta-spectacle. For example, Greeks and Trojans register joy and fear, respectively, when Ajax appears on the battlefield:

IL.7.214  τὸν δὲ καὶ Ἀργεῖοι μέγ' ἐγήθεον εἰσορόωντες,
IL.7.214  And the Argives looking upon him were made glad, while the Trojans
IL.7.215  Τρῶας δὲ τρόμος αἰνὸς ὑπήλυθε γυῖα ἕκαστον,
IL.7.215  were taken every man in the knees with trembling and terror,

Agamemnon and Menelaos both panic when they witness Menelaos' wound in Book 4, yet Menelaos revises his response to it once he discovers its relatively benign status:

IL.4.148  ῥίγησεν δ' ἄρ' ἔπειτα ἄναξ ἀνδρῶν Ἀγαμέμνων
IL.4.148  Agamemnon the lord of men was taken with shuddering
IL.4.149  ὡς εἶδεν μέλαν αἷμα καταρρέον ἐξ ὠτειλῆς:
IL.4.149  fear as he saw how from the cut the dark blood trickled downward,
IL.4.150  ῥίγησεν δὲ καὶ αὐτὸς ἀρηΐφιλος Μενέλαος.

---

[176] Cf. 3.342.
[177] Cf. 7.307.
[178] Cf. 14.441.
[179] Cf. 15.280.

IL.4.150 and Menelaos the warlike himself shuddered in terror;
IL.4.151 ὡς δὲ ἴδεν νεῦρόν τε καὶ ὄγκους ἐκτὸς ἐόντας
IL.4.151 but when he saw the binding strings and the hooked barbs outside
IL.4.152 ἄψορρόν οἱ θυμὸς ἐνὶ στήθεσσιν ἀγέρθη.
IL.4.152 the wound, his spirit was gathered again back into him.

Iliadic mortals also form meta-audiences to witness significant events such as the funeral games of Patroclus in Book 23 and Achilles' pursuit of Hector in Book 22, which Homer compares explicitly to an athletic contest, only, as Jasper Griffin puts it, "...the gods were among the audience, and the stake was the life of Hector."[180] The meta-theatrical element is essential to this scene, as the following passage makes clear:

IL.22.145 οἳ δὲ παρὰ σκοπιὴν καὶ ἐρινεὸν ἠνεμόεντα
IL.22.145 They raced along by the watching point and the windy fig tree
IL.22.146 τείχεος αἰὲν ὑπὲκ κατ' ἀμαξιτὸν ἐσσεύοντο,
IL.22.146 always away from under the wall and along the wagon-way

emphasizing the presence of meta-spectators and a sufficient distance between meta-spectacle and wall (ὑπὲκ) to accommodate meta-theatrical activity. The first meta-audience mentioned is the gods—all of them:

IL.22.165 ὣς τὼ τρὶς Πριάμοιο πόλιν πέρι δινηθήτην
IL.22.165 so these two swept whirling about the city of Priam
IL.22.166 καρπαλίμοισι πόδεσσι: θεοὶ δ' ἐς πάντες ὁρῶντο:
IL.22.166 in the speed of their feet, while all the gods were looking upon them.

The scene remains in Olympus, where Zeus, in a rare display of *aporia*, canvasses the other gods about what course of action to take and allows Athena to descend to the Trojan plain to assist Achilles against Hector. Before she arrives, the mortal meta-audience is introduced indirectly,[181] consistent with Homer's general tendency to present spatial information in the course of the action rather than in descriptive blocks that stanch the narrative flow:[182]

---

[180] 1978: 14.
[181] They are not explicitly said to watch until line 370, after Hector has been killed.
[182] Cf. Leach (1988: 32).

IL.22.205  λαοῖσιν δ' ἀνένευε καρήατι δῖος Ἀχιλλεύς,
IL.22.205  But brilliant Achilles kept shaking his head at his own people
IL.22.206  οὐδ' ἔα ἱέμεναι ἐπὶ Ἕκτορι πικρὰ βέλεμνα,
IL.22.206  and would not let them throw their bitter projectiles at Hector
IL.22.207  μή τις κῦδος ἄροιτο βαλών, ὃ δὲ δεύτερος ἔλθοι.
IL.22.207  for fear the thrower might win the glory, and himself come second.

This subtle detail suffices to give us a sense of watching the proceedings as meta-audience rather than primary audience, thus imbuing the scene with a correspondingly greater degree of emotional involvement. No sudden close-ups of specific meta-spectators is necessary to sustain this illusion, which has been achieved in a manner impossible to duplicate cinematically.[183] Ebert addresses this issue in his review of the movie "Troy":

As for the Greek cities themselves, a cliche from the old Hollywood epics has remained intact. This is the convention that whenever a battle of great drama takes place, all the important characters have box seats for it. When Achilles battles Hector before the walls of Troy, for example, Priam and his family have a sort of viewing stand right at the front of the palace, and we get the usual crowd reaction shots, some of them awkward closeups of actresses told to look grieved.[184]

In contrast with its prominent meta-theatrical function in the *Iliad*, Olympus is more often referred to than traveled to in the *Odyssey*. This reflects the terrestrial orientation of Odyssean action, focused more on Odysseus' linear trajectory toward Ithaka and his relationship with Athena than on the contrast between human and divine forces or the establishment of Olympus as a parallel dramatic theater. Homer stresses the open-endedness of Odyssean story space and its corresponding lack of *Iliad*-like constriction through frequent reference to the expansiveness of the sea[185] and its imperviousness to nautical swiftness;[186] of the

---

[183] If, for example, voice-over narration were provided to convey to the audience Achilles' motive for shaking his head, the audience would no longer be watching the scene through the eyes of the meta-spectators but rather of the primary narrator, whose perspective this observation would represent.

[184] 2004.

[185] Cf. *Od.* 3.321-22.

land,[187] its manifold regions,[188] and the vast distances between them;[189] of κλέος, with its awesome horizontal[190] and vertical[191] scope, and yet to the transcension of scenographic anarchy through courage,[192] friendship,[193] culture,[194] patriotism,[195] the gods' will,[196] and the power of supplication,[197] affirming the inherent formidability of Odyssean distances through the necessity to contain them within manageable limits. The exotic status of divine society in the *Odyssey* is underscored by the following description of Olympus, which lacks the familiar ring of comparable scenes in the *Iliad*, despite the extensive action situated there at the beginning of the previous book:

OD.6.41 ἡ μὲν ἄρ' ὣς εἰποῦσ' ἀπέβη γλαυκῶπις Ἀθήνη
OD.6.41 So the gray-eyed Athene spoke and went away from her
OD.6.42 Οὔλυμπόνδ', ὅθι φασὶ θεῶν ἕδος ἀσφαλὲς αἰεὶ
OD.6.42 to Olympus, where the abode of the gods stands firm and unmoving
OD.6.43 ἔμμεναι. οὔτ' ἀνέμοισι τινάσσεται οὔτε ποτ' ὄμβρῳ
OD.6.43 forever, they say, and is not shaken with winds nor spattered with rains,
OD.6.44 δεύεται οὔτε χιὼν ἐπιπίλναται, ἀλλὰ μάλ' αἴθρη
OD.6.44 nor does snow pile ever there, but the shining bright air
OD.6.45 πέπταται ἀννέφελος, λευκὴ δ' ἐπιδέδρομεν αἴγλη:
OD.6.45 stretches cloudless away, and the white light glances upon it.

In conformity with the terrestrial emphasis of the *Odyssey*, Athena tends to appear at ground level rather than in Olympus, functioning, not as a detached spectator, but as the main benefactor of Odysseus, Telemachus, and Penelope. When Telemachus prays to Athena in the following scene,

---

[186] Cf. *Od.* 4.708-09.
[187] Cf. *Od.* 4.602-03.
[188] Cf. *Od.* 14.120.
[189] Cf. *Od.* 4.757.
[190] Cf. *Od.* 4.726.
[191] Cf. *Od.* 9.20.
[192] Cf. *Od.* 7.51-2.
[193] Cf. *Od.* 9.16-18.
[194] Cf. *Od.* 9.273-74.
[195] Cf. *Od.* 9.34-6.
[196] Cf. *Od.* 3.231.
[197] Cf. *Od.* 6.310-12.

for example, she is characteristically ready at hand to offer him help:

OD.2.267 ὣς ἔφατ' εὐχόμενος, σχεδόθεν δέ οἱ ἦλθεν Ἀθήνη,
OD.2.267 So he spoke in prayer, and from nearby Athene came to him
OD.2.268 Μέντορι εἰδομένη ἠμὲν δέμας ἠδὲ καὶ αὐδήν,
OD.2.268 likening herself to Mentor in voice and appearance.

This synergy between Athena and her mortal beneficiaries is symbolized by the display of mortal/immortal synchronicity in the following passage:

OD.5.192 ὣς ἄρα φωνήσασ' ἡγήσατο δῖα θεάων
OD.5.192 So she spoke, a shining goddess, and led the way swiftly,
OD.5.193 καρπαλίμως· ὁ δ' ἔπειτα μετ' ἴχνια βαῖνε θεοῖο.
OD.5.193 and the man followed behind her walking in the god's footsteps.
OD.5.194 ἷξον δὲ σπεῖος γλαφυρὸν θεὸς ἠδὲ καὶ ἀνήρ,
OD.5.194 They made their way, the man and the god, to the hollow cavern,
OD.5.195 καί ῥ' ὁ μὲν ἔνθα καθέζετ' ἐπὶ θρόνου ἔνθεν ἀνέστη
OD.5.195 and he seated himself upon the chair from which Hermes lately
OD.5.196 Ἑρμείας, νύμφη δ' ἐτίθει πάρα πᾶσαν ἐδωδήν,
OD.5.196 had risen, while the nymph set all manner of food before him
OD.5.197 ἔσθειν καὶ πίνειν, οἷα βροτοὶ ἄνδρες ἔδουσιν·
OD.5.197 to eat and drink, such things as mortal people feed upon.

The two primary terrestrial meta-theaters of the *Iliad* are the Greek camp and the Trojan wall. In the following scene the Greek camp serves as an outpost for Agamemnon to survey the current situation before he encounters Nestor to plan an ambush of the Trojan camp. His view of Trojan territory, however, is not as comprehensive as that enjoyed by the gods in Olympus or Ida. He can only deduce the activity of the Trojans themselves through visual (12) and auditory (13) cues, while his access to the Greeks (14) and Olympus (16) is unrestricted:

IL.10.11 ἤτοι ὅτ' ἐς πεδίον τὸ Τρωϊκὸν ἀθρήσειε,
IL.10.11 Now he would gaze across the plain to the Trojan camp, wondering
IL.10.12 θαύμαζεν πυρὰ πολλὰ τὰ καίετο Ἰλιόθι πρὸ
IL.10.12 at the number of their fires that were burning in front of Ilion,
IL.10.13 αὐλῶν συρίγγων τ' ἐνοπὴν ὅμαδόν τ' ἀνθρώπων.
IL.10.13 toward the high calls of their flutes and pipes, the murmur of people.

IL.10.14   αὐτὰρ ὅτ' ἐς νῆάς τε ἴδοι καὶ λαὸν Ἀχαιῶν,

IL.10.14   Now as he would look again to the ships and the Achaian

IL.10.15   πολλὰς ἐκ κεφαλῆς προθελύμνους ἕλκετο χαίτας

IL.10.15   people, he would drag the hair by its roots from his head, looking

IL.10.16   ὑψόθ' ἐόντι Διί, μέγα δ' ἔστενε κυδάλιμον κῆρ.

IL.10.16   toward Zeus on high, and his proud heart was stricken with lamentation.

Once Achilles returns to his camp after his near-fatal argument with Agamemnon in Book 1, it becomes a meta-theater in its own right, providing an alternate view of the action from Achilles' ship,[198]

IL.11.599   τὸν δὲ ἰδὼν ἐνόησε ποδάρκης δῖος Ἀχιλλεύς:

IL.11.599   Now swift-footed brilliant Achilles saw him and watched him,

IL.11.600   εἱστήκει γὰρ ἐπὶ πρυμνῇ μεγακήτεϊ νηὶ

IL.11.600   for he was standing on the stern of his huge-hollowed vessel

IL.11.601   εἰσορόων πόνον αἰπὺν ἰῶκά τε δακρυόεσσαν.

IL.11.601   looking out over the sheer war work and the sorrowful onrush.

or from his shelter,

IL.10.11   ἤτοι ὅτ' ἐς πεδίον τὸ Τρωϊκὸν ἀθρήσειε,

IL.10.11   Now he would gaze across the plain to the Trojan camp, wondering

IL.10.12   θαύμαζεν πυρὰ πολλὰ τὰ καίετο Ἰλιόθι πρὸ

IL.10.12   at the number of their fires that were burning in front of Ilion,

IL.10.13   αὐλῶν συρίγγων τ' ἐνοπὴν ὅμαδόν τ' ἀνθρώπων.

IL.10.13   toward the high calls of their flutes and pipes, the murmur of people.

IL.10.14   αὐτὰρ ὅτ' ἐς νῆάς τε ἴδοι καὶ λαὸν Ἀχαιῶν,

IL.10.14   Now as he would look again to the ships and the Achaian

IL.10.15   πολλὰς ἐκ κεφαλῆς προθελύμνους ἕλκετο χαίτας

IL.10.15   people, he would drag the hair by its roots from his head, looking

IL.10.16   ὑψόθ' ἐόντι Διί, μέγα δ' ἔστενε κυδάλιμον κῆρ.

IL.10.16   toward Zeus on high, and his proud heart was stricken with lamentation.

complementing the Greek camp proper the way Ida complements Olympus, providing an alternative perspective on the military action. Likewise, the Trojan wall constitutes the Trojan equivalent to Achilles' shelter in its spatial relationship to Troy proper. On the other hand, Troy, unlike the Greek camp (its scenographic antipode) does not itself offer a

---

[198] Cf. Kuntz (1993: 9).

view of the battlefield, and thus the Trojans are limited to the single perspective provided by the Trojan wall. This meta-theatrical contrast between Greek and Trojan armies emphasizes the vulnerability of the Greek ships and the relative security of the city. It also provides the opportunity to dramatize the act of meta-spectatorship itself. For example, Andromache's distance from the main action is most clear in Book 22, when she eventually learns of Hector's death. Hecuba mourns outside but Andromache does not yet hear her:

IL.22.437    ὣς ἔφατο κλαίουσ', ἄλοχος δ' οὔ πώ τι πέπυστο
IL.22.437    So she spoke in tears but the wife of Hector had not yet
IL.22.438    Ἕκτορος: οὐ γάρ οἵ τις ἐτήτυμος ἄγγελος ἐλθὼν
IL.22.438    heard: for no sure messenger had come to her and told her
IL.22.439    ἤγγειλ' ὅττί ῥά οἱ πόσις ἔκτοθι μίμνε πυλάων,
IL.22.439    how her husband had held his ground there outside the gates;

Her isolation is dramatized by the contrast between the emotional devastation outside and her own calm demeanor inside:

IL.22.440    ἀλλ' ἥ γ' ἱστὸν ὕφαινε μυχῷ δόμου ὑψηλοῖο
IL.22.440    but she was weaving a web in the inner room of the high house,
IL.22.441    δίπλακα πορφυρέην, ἐν δὲ θρόνα ποικίλ' ἔπασσε.
IL.22.441    a red folding robe, and inworking elaborate figures.
IL.22.442    κέκλετο δ' ἀμφιπόλοισιν ἐϋπλοκάμοις κατὰ δῶμα
IL.22.442    She called out through the house to her lovely-haired handmaidens
IL.22.443    ἀμφὶ πυρὶ στῆσαι τρίποδα μέγαν, ὄφρα πέλοιτο
IL.22.443    to set a great cauldron over the fire, so that there would be
IL.22.444    Ἕκτορι θερμὰ λοετρὰ μάχης ἐκ νοστήσαντι
IL.22.444    hot water for Hector's bath as he came back out of the fighting;
IL.22.445    νηπίη, οὐδ' ἐνόησεν ὅ μιν μάλα τῆλε λοετρῶν
IL.22.445    poor innocent, nor knew how, far from waters for bathing,
IL.22.446    χερσὶν Ἀχιλλῆος δάμασε γλαυκῶπις Ἀθήνη.
IL.22.446    Pallas Athene had cut him down at the hands of Achilles.

Yet she suspects that something is not quite right once she hears the crying:

IL.22.447    κωκυτοῦ δ' ἤκουσε καὶ οἰμωγῆς ἀπὸ πύργου:
IL.22.447    She heard from the great bastion the noise of mourning and sorrow.

We cut suddenly to an object that falls from her hand to the ground,

IL.22.448   τῆς δ' ἐλελίχθη γυῖα, χαμαὶ δέ οἱ ἔκπεσε κερκίς:
IL.22.448   Her limbs spun, and the shuttle dropped from her hand to the ground.

a powerful visual technique[199] reminiscent of the opening scene from "Citizen Kane":

> DISSOLVE: INT. KANE'S BEDROOM - FAINT DAWN - 1940
> A snow scene. An incredible one. Big, impossible flakes of snow, a too picturesque farmhouse and a snow man. The jingling of sleigh bells in the musical score now makes an ironic reference to Indian Temple bells - the music freezes -
>
> KANE'S OLD OLD VOICE
> Rosebud...
>
> The camera pulls back, showing the whole scene to be contained in one of those glass balls which are sold in novelty stores all over the world. A hand - Kane's hand, which has been holding the ball, relaxes. The ball falls out of his hand and bounds down two carpeted steps leading to the bed, the camera following. The ball falls off the last step onto the marble floor where it breaks, the fragments glittering in the first rays of the morning sun.

The suspense builds when Andromache calls her handmaidens and orders them to accompany her to the Trojan wall to determine whether the noise, as she suspects, is a sign of Hector's slaying at the hands of Achilles. The intensity is increased by her urgency as she bursts out of her house and approaches the wall:

IL.22.460   ὣς φαμένη μεγάροιο διέσσυτο μαινάδι ἴση
IL.22.460   So she spoke, and ran out of the house like a raving woman
IL.22.461   παλλομένη κραδίην: ἅμα δ' ἀμφίπολοι κίον αὐτῇ
IL.22.461   with pulsing heart, and her two handmaidens went along with her.

Even when she arrives at the wall, however, her ignorance is dispelled only gradually, as she searches (παπτήνασ') for Hector,

---

[199] Cf. Münsterberg (1970: 48).

IL.22.462 αὐτὰρ ἐπεὶ πύργόν τε καὶ ἀνδρῶν ἷξεν ὅμιλον
IL.22.462 But when she came to the bastion and where the men were gathered
IL.22.463 ἔστη παπτήνασ' ἐπὶ τείχεϊ,
IL.22.463 she stopped, staring, on the wall;

until finally, at the end of line 463, she perceives him:

IL.22.463 τὸν δ' ἐνόησεν
IL.22.463 and she saw him

It is at this moment, after twenty-five lines in which Andromache gradually emerges from the labyrinthine interiors of Troy, that she becomes a meta-spectator in her own right, equipped with visual access to the action below, which constitutes both meta-spectacle to her ·and second-order meta-spectacle to us, as we watch the sort of scene to which we are normally granted direct access, but which gains dramatic force as we see it through Andromache's eyes:

IL.22.464 ἑλκόμενον πρόσθεν πόλιος: ταχέες δέ μιν ἵπποι
IL.22.464 being dragged in front of the city, and the running horses
IL.22.465 ἔλκον ἀκηδέστως κοίλας ἐπὶ νῆας Ἀχαιῶν.
IL.22.465 dragged him at random toward the hollow ships of the Achaians.

The narrator then shifts our attention from meta-spectacle to meta-spectator through an extreme close-up of Andromache's eyes themselves,

IL.22.466 τὴν δὲ κατ' ὀφθαλμῶν ἐρεβεννὴ νὺξ ἐκάλυψεν,
IL.22.466 The darkness of night misted over the eyes of Andromache.

achieving a pathetic effect similar to when the Greeks witnessed their ships being overrun by Trojans in Book 13:

IL.13.86 καί σφιν ἄχος κατὰ θυμὸν ἐγίνετο δερκομένοισι
IL.13.86 discouragement of the heart came over them, as they watched
IL.13.87 Τρῶας, τοὶ μέγα τεῖχος ὑπερκατέβησαν ὁμίλῳ.
IL.13.87 the Trojans, and how in a mass they had overswarmed the great wall.
IL.13.88 τοὺς οἵ γ' εἰσορόωντες ὑπ' ὀφρύσι δάκρυα λεῖβον:

102

IL.13.88   As they saw them the tears dripped from their eyes.

While decomposition transports the audience into the action along the z axis of the spatial continuum, and intercutting keeps them at bay as they watch the characters on the Trojan plain merge toward a common center, meta-audience transports them instantaneously within the mind of a character and shows them the world through his or her eyes. Thus, unlike the previous two devices, meta-audience dictates, not merely active or passive reception on the part of the audience but rather an actual transformation, however temporary, of their very identity. This complicates their relationship with both the story and the discourse, indeed threatens to obliterate the boundaries between them, as the transition between lines 87 and 88 of Book 13 makes especially clear, during which the audience is suddenly thrust back into their role as real-world spectators following three lines in which they look subjectively through the very eyes they now perceive objectively at close-up range. In the final chapter we consider a device that, like meta-audience, requires us to assume the vision of a given character, only in this case we see, not through his or her *eyes*, but through his or her *imagination*.

# CHAPTER FIVE

# VIGNETTE

"Throughout [the *Iliad*] flashlike perspectives open up beyond the action." (Vivante, 1995: 74)

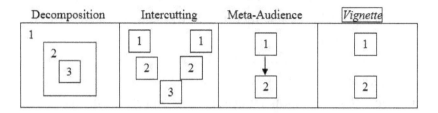

| Decomposition | Intercutting | Meta-Audience | *Vignette* |
|---|---|---|---|

Vignette occurs when the action suddenly shifts to an area that was previously offscreen.[200] Seymour Stern attributes the device to D.W. Griffith,[201] yet Griffith himself acknowledges its literary provenience.[202] Its theatrical counterpart, the offstage excursion, functions somewhat similarly, providing information, actual or hypothetical, in the present, past, or future, about a location distant from the central scene at hand.[203] The difference in media between cinema and theater, however, dictates the correspondingly distinctive manner in which each art form executes offscreen and offstage action, respectively. Excursions to the offstage in theater are left solely to the imagination of the audience to visualize, relying upon language to refer to an invisible scene parallel to the scene portrayed physically before them.[204] Excursions to the offscreen in cinema, on the other hand, differ from their theatrical counterpart in the immediacy they share with the main spectacle, presenting the offscreen action before the eyes of the viewer rather than hypothetically through words. In epic, because words are used as its exclusive medium rather

---

[200] Cf. Aumont et al. (1992: 12); Lessing (1984: 66).

[201] 1979: 65-6.

[202] Cf. Griffith (1925: 66); Münsterberg (1970: 45).

[203] Scolnicov (1987: 13-14).

[204] Cf. Lieblein (1986: 120); Scolnicov (1987: 13); Longman (1987: 151).

than, as in theater, in competition with scenography, excursions to distant regions are no less capable of *enargeia* than the main action they temporarily diverge from. Thus they function more like the offscreen of film than like the offstage of theater, despite the identical verbal medium used in epic and theater.[205] Therefore, the Elsewhere,[206] the verbal equivalent to the offscreen region, constitutes, not merely an invisible realm possessing exclusively referential existence, but rather a dramatic arena in its own right, no less potentially vivid and contextualized than the main action itself.

To get a clearer sense of what constitutes vignette, we should first consider certain constructions which, while similar to it in one way or another, do not strictly speaking qualify as legitimate excursions to the Elsewhere. A transition between two locations, for example, can achieve an effect similar to vignette, as in Book 3 when the scene shifts from Paris and Helen in the rarified atmosphere of Paris' bedroom to the Trojan plain:

IL.3.448 τὼ μὲν ἄρ' ἐν τρητοῖσι κατεύνασθεν λεχέεσσιν,
IL.3.448 So these two were laid in the carven bed. But Atreides
IL.3.449 Ἀτρείδης δ' ἀν' ὅμιλον ἐφοίτα θηρὶ ἐοικὼς
IL.3.449 ranged like a wild beast up and down the host, to discover
IL.3.450 εἴ που ἐσαθρήσειεν Ἀλέξανδρον θεοειδέα.
IL.3.450 whether he could find anywhere godlike Alexandros.

Because we do not return back to the original location, however, this transition does not constitute an instance of vignette proper. In order to qualify as vignette, the scenographic element must be concrete, situating the characters in a perceptual rather than merely conceptual framework. Thus, when Diomedes kills Xanthos and Thoön in Book 5, the description of their father's future bereavement is less pathetic than if the scene were set in a particular location to increase its dramatic verisimilitude:

---

[205] Balutowa (1979: 114-15); Frazier (1999: 453).
[206] Lyons (1991: 72).

IL.5.155 ἔνθ' ὅ γε τοὺς ἐνάριζε, φίλον δ' ἐξαίνυτο θυμὸν
IL.5.155 There he killed these two and took away the dear life from them
IL.5.156 ἀμφοτέρω, πατέρι δὲ γόον καὶ κήδεα λυγρὰ
IL.5.156 both, leaving to their father lamentation and sorrowful
IL.5.157 λεῖπ', ἐπεὶ οὐ ζώοντε μάχης ἐκνοστήσαντε
IL.5.157 affliction, since he was not to welcome them home from the fighting
IL.5.158 δέξατο: χηρωσταὶ δὲ διὰ κτῆσιν δατέοντο.
IL.5.158 alive still; and remoter kinsmen shared his possessions.

Furthermore, the mere fact that something is lying somewhere else does not convey the same experience as the actual image of that object lying there, since it lacks the element of *enargeia* indispensible to vignette.[207] For example, in Book 23 Achilles refers to a corselet that he has Automedon retrieve from his shelter:

IL.23.558 Ἀντίλοχ', εἰ μὲν δή με κελεύεις οἴκοθεν ἄλλοIL.23.558
IL.23.558 'Antilochos, if you would have me bring some other thing out of my dwelling
IL.23.559 Εὐμήλῳ ἐπιδοῦναι, ἐγὼ δέ κε καὶ τὸ τελέσσω.
IL.23.559 as special gift for Eumelos, then for your sake I will do it.
IL.23.560 δώσω οἱ θώρηκα, τὸν Ἀστεροπαῖον ἀπηύρων
IL.23.560 I will give him that corselet I stripped from Asteropaios;
IL.23.561 χάλκεον, ᾧ πέρι χεῦμα φαεινοῦ κασσιτέροιο
IL.23.561 it is bronze, but there is an overlay circled about it
IL.23.562 ἀμφιδεδίνηται: πολέος δέ οἱ ἄξιος ἔσται.
IL.23.562 in shining tin. It will be a gift that will mean much to him.'

It is not, however, until the corselet itself appears in line 565, when Automedon puts it in Achilles' hands, that we perceive it *in situ*:

IL.23.563 ἦ ῥα, καὶ Αὐτομέδοντι φίλῳ ἐκέλευσεν ἑταίρῳ
IL.23.563 He spoke, and told Automedon, his beloved companion,
IL.23.564 οἰσέμεναι κλισίηθεν: ὃ δ' ᾤχετο καί οἱ ἔνεικεν,
IL.23.564 to bring it out of the shelter, and he went away, and brought it back,
IL.23.565 Εὐμήλῳ δ' ἐν χερσὶ τίθει: ὃ δὲ δέξατο χαίρων.
IL.23.565 and put it in Eumelos' hands. And he accepted it joyfully

Although οἴκοθεν is mentioned in line 558, the fact that the corselet is located in Achilles' shelter is not the same as *seeing* it located there,

---

[207] Cf. Suvin (1987: 313).

regardless of how thoroughly detailed its description. For the focus of vignette is not merely on the object in question, nor on its location, but rather on the symbiosis between the two. Thus, because we do not perceive the corselet in a parallel location but rather in the same location as Achilles himself, the passage does not constitute vignette but rather a close-up view of the object in question which, until line 565, possesses a strictly conceptual provenience.

Vignette provides the audience with a temporary simile-like escape[208] from the closed story space of the *Iliad*, varying the presentation of the narrative in much the way that the diversification of focal distances achieves,[209] only rather than alternating between long shots and close-ups we alternate between the here-and-now, on the one hand, and the there-and-now or the there-and-then, on the other. Homer shares with the playwright the tendency to transcend the constrictive confines of closed story space. According to Colin Duckworth, for example, the plays of Beckett exploit "the austerity of the stage space," drawing upon "the rich evocation of worlds elsewhere."[210] And Michael Issacharoff observes that the more constrictive the story space is, the more significant the offstage region becomes, while a relatively open story space tends to marginalize the offstage region or at best to relegate it to "a single described area."[211] Indeed, Homeric space corroborates Issacharoff's theory: whereas the closed story space of the *Iliad* inspires a great variety of Elsewhere activity,[212] the open story space of the *Odyssey* limits itself primarily to a single region of the Elsewhere (Ithaka) toward which the action constantly gravitates. It is worth considering how Homer employs vignette in the *Odyssey* in this overtly linear, plot-centered manner before turning to its Iliadic counterpart, according to which each individual instance of the device exhibits a dramatic self-sufficiency whose thematic coherence becomes clear only

---

[208] Cf. Bowra (1972: 60).

[209] Münsterberg (1970: 41).

[210] 1990: 131.

[211] 1981: 222.

[212] This tendency is shared by tragedy, cf. Scolnikov (1987: 16-17).

through synchronic analysis.

Near the beginning of the *Odyssey*, the whereabouts of Odysseus are established in a conversation between Zeus and Athena, in which Athena expresses her concern for, and reveals the location of, the Greek hero:

OD.1.48   ἀλλά μοι ἀμφ' Ὀδυσῆι δαΐφρονι δαίεται ἦτορ,
OD.1.48   But the heart in me is torn for the sake of wise Odysseus,
OD.1.49   δυσμόρῳ, ὃς δὴ δηθὰ φίλων ἄπο πήματα πάσχει
OD.1.49   unhappy man, who still, far from his friends, is suffering
OD.1.50   νήσῳ ἐν ἀμφιρύτῃ, ὅθι τ' ὀμφαλός ἐστι θαλάσσης.
OD.1.50   griefs, on the sea-washed island, the navel of all the waters,
OD.1.51   νῆσος δενδρήεσσα, θεὰ δ' ἐν δώματα ναίει,
OD.1.51   a wooded island, and there a goddess has made her dwelling place

When Athena visits Telemachus to inform him about Odysseus, Telemachus expresses, not merely uncertainty about his father's whereabouts, but his belief that he is dead:

OD.1.158   ξεῖνε φίλ', εἰ καὶ μοι νεμεσήσεαι ὅττι κεν εἴπω;
OD.1.158   Dear stranger, would you be scandalized at what I say to you?
OD.1.159   τούτοισιν μὲν ταῦτα μέλει, κίθαρις καὶ ἀοιδή,
OD.1.159   This is all they think of, the lyre and the singing. Easy
OD.1.160   ῥεῖ', ἐπεὶ ἀλλότριον βίοτον νήποινον ἔδουσιν,
OD.1.160   for them, since without penalty they eat up the substance
OD.1.161   ἀνέρος, οὗ δή που λεύκ' ὀστέα πύθεται ὄμβρῳ
OD.1.161   of a man whose white bones lie out in the rain and fester
OD.1.162   κείμεν' ἐπ' ἠπείρου, ἢ εἰν ἁλὶ κῦμα κυλίνδει.
OD.1.162   somewhere on the mainland, or roll in the wash of the breakers.

At this point Telemachus establishes Ithaka as the central hub of the Odyssean Elsewhere, despite the hypothetical state of his present knowledge:

OD.1.163   εἰ κεῖνόν γ' Ἰθάκηνδε ἰδοίατο νοστήσαντα,
OD.1.163   If they were ever to see him coming back to Ithaka
OD.1.164   πάντες κ' ἀρησαίατ' ἐλαφρότεροι πόδας εἶναι
OD.1.164   all the prayer of them all would be to be lighter on their feet
OD.1.165   ἢ ἀφνειότεροι χρυσοῖό τε ἐσθῆτός τε.
OD.1.165   instead of to be richer men for gold and clothing.

Then Athena, disguised as Mentes, informs Telemachus of the fact that his father is still alive, already known to the audience through her conversation with Zeus:

OD.1.196  οὐ γάρ πω τέθνηκεν ἐπὶ χθονὶ δῖος Ὀδυσσεύς,
OD.1.196  For no death on the land has befallen the great Odysseus,
OD.1.197  ἀλλ' ἔτι που ζωὸς κατερύκεται εὐρέι πόντῳ
OD.1.197  But somewhere, alive on the wide sea, he is held captive,
OD.1.198  νήσῳ ἐν ἀμφιρύτῃ, χαλεποὶ δέ μιν ἄνδρες ἔχουσιν
OD.1.198  on a sea-washed island, and savage men have him in their keeping,
OD.1.199  ἄγριοι, οἵ που κεῖνον ἐρυκανόωσ' ἀέκοντα.
OD.1.199  rough men, who somehow keep him back, though he is unwilling.

Thus, Odysseus' existence becomes factual rather than hypothetical to Telemachus, whose uncertainty now hinges exclusively upon his father's location, the knowledge about which Athena encourages him to ascertain, thereby establishing the central *telos* of the *Odyssey*: the expulsion of the suitors from, and the subsequent resacralization of, Odysseus' palace:

OD.1.253  ὢ πόποι, ἦ δὴ πολλὸν ἀποιχομένου Ὀδυσῆος
OD.1.253  Oh, for shame. How great your need is now of the absent
OD.1.254  δεύῃ, ὅ κεν μνηστῆρσιν ἀναιδέσι χεῖρας ἐφείη.
OD.1.254  Odysseus, who would lay his hands on these shameless suitors.
OD.1.255  εἰ γὰρ νῦν ἐλθὼν δόμου ἐν πρώτῃσι θύρῃσι
OD.1.255  I wish he could come now to stand in the outer doorway
OD.1.256  σταίη, ἔχων πήληκα καὶ ἀσπίδα καὶ δύο δοῦρε,
OD.1.256  of his house, wearing a helmet and carrying shield and two spears,
OD.1.257  τοῖος ἐὼν οἷόν μιν ἐγὼ τὰ πρῶτ' ἐνόησα
OD.1.257  the way he was the first time that ever I saw him
OD.1.258  οἴκῳ ἐν ἡμετέρῳ πίνοντά τε τερπόμενόν τε,
OD.1.258  in our own house, drinking his wine and taking his pleasure,

The fact that Telemachus is now aware of Odysseus' existence, however, does not mean that this knowledge automatically extends to the other characters as well. In fact, once Telemachus partakes in privileged knowledge about Odysseus, the other mortals continue to harbor the same illusions about Odysseus' fate as Telemachus previously did. Penelope, for example, remains ignorant of Odysseus' existence until the dramatic recognition scene in Book 23:

OD.4.722 κλῦτε, φίλαι: πέρι γάρ μοι Ὀλύμπιος ἄλγε' ἔδωκεν
OD.4.722 Hear me, dear friends. The Olympian has given me sorrows
OD.4.723 ἐκ πασέων, ὅσσαι μοι ὁμοῦ τράφεν ἠδ' ἐγένοντο:
OD.4.723 beyond all others who were born and brought up together
OD.4.724 ἢ πρὶν μὲν πόσιν ἐσθλὸν ἀπώλεσα θυμολέοντα,
OD.4.724 with me, for first I lost a husband with the heart of a lion
OD.4.725 παντοίης ἀρετῇσι κεκασμένον ἐν Δαναοῖσιν,
OD.4.725 and who among the Danaans surpassed in all virtues,
OD.4.726 ἐσθλόν, τοῦ κλέος εὐρὺ καθ' Ἑλλάδα καὶ μέσον Ἄργος.
OD.4.726 and great, whose fame goes wide through Hellas and midmost Argos

This results in two parallel versions of the Elsewhere according to which Odysseus is either dead or alive, depending upon the knowledge of the speaker at a given dramatic juncture. The latter is expressed in two ways: by characters, beginning with Telemachus and followed by those who subsequently recognize Odysseus, evoking Ithaka as the future site of dramatic conflict and resolution, and by Odysseus himself, as in Book 5, when he informs Calypso that despite her beauty he nevertheless longs for Penelope and his Ithakan palace:

OD.5.219 ἀλλὰ καὶ ὣς ἐθέλω καὶ ἐέλδομαι ἤματα πάντα
OD.5.219 But even so, what I want and all my days I pine for
OD.5.220 οἴκαδέ τ' ἐλθέμεναι καὶ νόστιμον ἦμαρ ἰδέσθαι.
OD.5.220 is to go back to my house and see my day of homecoming.
OD.5.221 εἰ δ' αὖ τις ῥαίῃσι θεῶν ἐνὶ οἴνοπι πόντῳ,
OD.5.221 And if some god batters me far out on the wine-blue water,
OD.5.222 τλήσομαι ἐν στήθεσσιν ἔχων ταλαπενθέα θυμόν:
OD.5.222 I will endure it, keeping a stubborn spirit inside me,
OD.5.223 ἤδη γὰρ μάλα πόλλ' ἔπαθον καὶ πόλλ' ἐμόγησα
OD.5.223 for already I have suffered much and done much hard work
OD.5.224 κύμασι καὶ πολέμῳ: μετὰ καὶ τόδε τοῖσι γενέσθω.
OD.5.224 on the waves and in the fighting. So let this adventure follow.

In either case, the Ithakan Elsewhere remains the primary focus of the *Odyssey* until the action switches to Odysseus' palace. As we shall now see, this plot-centered approach to vignette in the *Odyssey* contrasts significantly from its Iliadic counterpart.

111

Each instance of vignette in the *Iliad* comprises a kind of mini-narrative, replete with meta-narrator, meta-narratee, and meta-protagonist. Although the Elsewhere is usually evoked by a character, the meta-narrator is sometimes identical with the primary narrator, transporting the audience to various sites of the Elsewhere in his own voice. He may, for instance, portray a fallen warrior's wife, contrasting the intimacy of the emotional bond between the two characters with the vast geographical distance between them:

IL.11.241  ὣς ὃ μὲν αὖθι πεσὼν κοιμήσατο χάλκεον ὕπνον
IL.11.241  So Iphidamas fell there and went into the brazen slumber,
IL.11.242  οἰκτρὸς ἀπὸ μνηστῆς ἀλόχου, ἀστοῖσιν ἀρήγων,
IL.11.242  unhappy, who came to help his own people, and left his young wife
IL.11.243  κουριδίης, ἧς οὔ τι χάριν ἴδε, πολλὰ δ' ἔδωκε:
IL.11.243  a bride, and had known no delight from her yet, and given much for her.

The narrator by no means limits himself to the past, however, when he employs vignette for pathetic effect. He may also exploit the present, as when Andromache is depicted in her room, still impervious to the death of Hector in lines 437-42 of Book 22, or even the future, as when Zeus weeps about, not what has happened or what is happening, but rather about what is going to happen to his son Sarpedon:

IL.16.459  αἱματοέσσας δὲ ψιάδας κατέχευεν ἔραζε
IL.16.459  He wept tears of blood that fell to the ground, for the sake
IL.16.460  παῖδα φίλον τιμῶν, τόν οἱ Πάτροκλος ἔμελλε
IL.16.460  of his beloved son, whom now Patroclus was presently
IL.16.461  φθίσειν ἐν Τροίῃ ἐριβώλακι τηλόθι πάτρης.
IL.16.461  to kill, by generous Troy and far from the land of his fathers.

This pathetic function of vignette is deployed extensively in Book 2 in the Catalogue of Ships. Besides the evocation of Protesilaos' wife in Phylake (699-702) and of the unfortunate Philoktetes in Lemnos (721-25), two vignettes focus on Achilles and the Myrmidons. The first occurs when Achilles' ship is mentioned along with the others. It is relatively abstract, emphasizing the reasons for Achilles' current inactivity more than the visualization of the scene itself:

IL.2.688   κεῖτο γὰρ ἐν νήεσσι ποδάρκης δῖος Ἀχιλλεὺς
IL.2.688   since he, swift-footed brilliant Achilles, lay where the ships were,
IL.2.689   κούρης χωόμενος Βρισηΐδος ἠϋκόμοιο,
IL.2.689   angered over the girl of the lovely hair, Briseis,
IL.2.690   τὴν ἐκ Λυρνησσοῦ ἐξείλετο πολλὰ μογήσας
IL.2.690   whom after much hard work he had taken away from Lyrnessos
IL.2.691   Λυρνησσὸν διαπορθήσας καὶ τείχεα Θήβης,
IL.2.691   after he had sacked Lyrnessos and the walls of Thebe
IL.2.692   κὰδ δὲ Μύνητ' ἔβαλεν καὶ Ἐπίστροφον ἐγχεσιμώρους,
IL.2.692   and struck down Epistrophos and Mynes the furious spearmen,
IL.2.693   υἱέας Εὐηνοῖο Σεληπιάδαο ἄνακτος:
IL.2.693   children of Euenos, king, and son of Selepios.
IL.2.694   τῆς ὅ γε κεῖτ' ἀχέων, τάχα δ' ἀνστήσεσθαι ἔμελλεν.
IL.2.694   For her sake he lay grieving now, but was soon to rise up.

In lines 721-25, however, when Achilles is mentioned again, in connection with Ajax as the second greatest Greek warrior after himself, the narrator paints a more vivid picture of the scene at Achilles' camp, thereby dramatizing rather than merely describing its almost idyllic isolation:

IL.2.771   ἀλλ' ὃ μὲν ἐν νήεσσι κορωνίσι ποντοπόροισι
IL.2.771   But Achilles lay apart among his curved sea-wandering
IL.2.772   κεῖτ' ἀπομηνίσας Ἀγαμέμνονι ποιμένι λαῶν
IL.2.772   vessels, raging at Agamemnon, the shepherd of the people,
IL.2.773   Ἀτρεΐδῃ: λαοὶ δὲ παρὰ ῥηγμῖνι θαλάσσης
IL.2.773   Atreus' son; and his men beside the break of the sea-beach
IL.2.774   δίσκοισιν τέρποντο καὶ αἰγανέῃσιν ἱέντες
IL.2.774   amused themselves with discs and with light spears for throwing
IL.2.775   τόξοισίν θ': ἵπποι δὲ παρ' ἅρμασιν οἷσιν ἕκαστος
IL.2.775   and bows; and the horses, standing each beside his chariot,
IL.2.776   λωτὸν ἐρεπτόμενοι ἐλεόθρεπτόν τε σέλινον
IL.2.776   champed their clover and the parsley that grows in wet places,
IL.2.777   ἕστασαν: ἅρματα δ' εὖ πεπυκασμένα κεῖτο ἀνάκτων
IL.2.777   resting, while the chariots of their lords stood covered
IL.2.778   ἐν κλισίῃς: οἳ δ' ἀρχὸν ἀρηΐφιλον ποθέοντες
IL.2.778   in the shelters, and the men forlorn of their warlike leader
IL.2.779   φοίτων ἔνθα καὶ ἔνθα κατὰ στρατὸν οὐδ' ἐμάχοντο.
IL.2.779   wandered here and there in the camp, and did no fighting.

The freedom of characters to transport the audience to the offstage region of the *Iliad* supplies them with a kind of meta-narrative power,

113

reciprocating the audience's pseudo-diegetic function as meta-audience with their own pseudo-extradiegetic function as meta-narrators. As such they possess the ability, alongside the narrator, to exert control over the audience's attention. This establishes them as formidable narrative agents in their own right (no less conspicuously so than Odysseus in the *Odyssey*) and the Elsewhere as a kind of spatial underground to which the audience is granted access through the will, not of the narrator (as with excursions to Olympus), but rather of the characters themselves. In their capacity as meta-narrators the characters who engage in vignette reveal a semantic dimension of the *Iliad* otherwise inaccessible to the audience, a sphere of meaning both complementary to yet independent from the main action.

Some excursions to the Elsewhere provide imaginary access to nostalgic venues. In Book 1, for example, Agamemnon evokes his home in Argos to illustrate, with great rhetorical persuasiveness, the future that awaits Briseis after the war as a result of Achilles' insistence that he relinquish Chryseis:

IL.1.29  τὴν δ' ἐγὼ οὐ λύσω: πρίν μιν καὶ γῆρας ἔπεισιν

IL.1.29  The girl I will not give back; sooner will old age come upon her

IL.1.30  ἡμετέρῳ ἐνὶ οἴκῳ ἐν Ἄργεϊ τηλόθι πάτρης

IL.1.30  in my own house, in Argos, far from her own land, going

IL.1.31  ἱστὸν ἐποιχομένην καὶ ἐμὸν λέχος ἀντιόωσαν:

IL.1.31  up and down by the loom and being in my bed as my companion.

In response to Agamemnon, Achilles paints an even more vivid picture of his own homeland to justify his imminent desertion of the war:

IL.1.152  οὐ γὰρ ἐγὼ Τρώων ἕνεκ' ἤλυθον αἰχμητάων

IL.1.152  I for my part did not come here for the sake of the Trojan

IL.1.153  δεῦρο μαχησόμενος, ἐπεὶ οὔ τί μοι αἴτιοί εἰσιν:

IL.1.153  spearmen to fight against them, since to me they have done nothing.

IL.1.154  οὐ γὰρ πώ ποτ' ἐμὰς βοῦς ἤλασαν οὐδὲ μὲν ἵππους,

IL.1.154  Never yet have they driven away my cattle or my horses,

IL.1.155  οὐδέ ποτ' ἐν Φθίῃ ἐριβώλακι βωτιανείρῃ

IL.1.155  never in Phthia where the soil is rich and men grow great did they

IL.1.156  καρπὸν ἐδηλήσαντ', ἐπεὶ ἦ μάλα πολλὰ μεταξὺ

IL.1.156  spoil my harvest, since indeed there is much that lies between us,

IL.1.157 οὔρεά τε σκιόεντα θάλασσά τε ἠχήεσσα:
IL.1.157 the shadowy mountains and the echoing sea; but for your sake,
IL.1.158 ἀλλὰ σοὶ ὦ μέγ' ἀναιδὲς ἅμ' ἑσπόμεθ' ὄφρα σὺ χαίρῃς,
IL.1.158 o great shamelessness, we followed, to do you favour,

This initiates a battle of wits between Achilles and Agamemnon that, as we shall see below, plays itself out in the arena of the Elsewhere.

Excursions to the Elsewhere provide an opportunity for characters who are otherwise denied access to certain locations to travel to them imaginatively, thereby creating dramatic situations based upon hypothetical rather than actual reality. This denial of access can be due to the character being on the opposite side of the war, as when Priam evokes Greece (4.90-2) or Agamemnon evokes Troy:

IL.4.169 ἀλλά μοι αἰνὸν ἄχος σέθεν ἔσσεται ὦ Μενέλαε
IL.4.169 But I shall suffer a terrible grief for you, Menelaos,
IL.4.170 αἴ κε θάνῃς καὶ μοῖραν ἀναπλήσῃς βιότοιο.
IL.4.170 if you die and fill out the destiny of your lifetime.
IL.4.171 καί κεν ἐλέγχιστος πολυδίψιον Ἄργος ἱκοίμην:
IL.4.171 And I must return a thing of reproach to Argos the thirsty,
IL.4.172 αὐτίκα γὰρ μνήσονται Ἀχαιοὶ πατρίδος αἴης:
IL.4.172 for now at once the Achaians will remember the land of their fathers;
IL.4.173 κὰδ δέ κεν εὐχωλὴν Πριάμῳ καὶ Τρωσὶ λίποιμεν
IL.4.173 and thus we would leave to Priam and to the Trojans Helen
IL.4.174 Ἀργείην Ἑλένην: σέο δ' ὀστέα πύσει ἄρουρα
IL.4.174 of Argos, to glory over, while the bones of you rot in the ploughland
IL.4.175 κειμένου ἐν Τροίῃ ἀτελευτήτῳ ἐπὶ ἔργῳ.
IL.4.175 as you lie dead in Troy, on a venture that went unaccomplished.

It can also consist of a hero evoking a location on the same side of battle, but which would nevertheless constitute an invasion of privacy if visited directly. When Thersites chastizes Agamemnon for not sticking to his initial plan to desert the war, for example, he violates his personal space by presuming to describe the scene within his inner sanctum:

IL.2.225 Ἀτρεΐδη τέο δ' αὖτ' ἐπιμέμφεαι ἠδὲ χατίζεις;
IL.2.225 'Son of Atreus, what thing further do you want, or find fault with
IL.2.226 πλεῖαί τοι χαλκοῦ κλισίαι, πολλαὶ δὲ γυναῖκες
IL.2.226 now? Your shelters are filled with bronze, there are plenty of the choicest

IL.2.227  εἰσὶν ἐνὶ κλισίης ἐξαίρετοι, ἅς τοι Ἀχαιοὶ
IL.2.227  women for you within your shelter, whom we Achaians

Just as vignette can transport characters themselves to locations otherwise inaccessible to them, so it enables them to envision other characters in imaginary situations made possible exclusively through their meta-narrative function. A character may, for example, involve his interlocutor in a hypothetical scenario, as when Zeus taunts Hera about her unquenchable loyalty to the Greeks:

IL.4.34  εἰ δὲ σύ γ' εἰσελθοῦσα πύλας καὶ τείχεα μακρὰ
IL.4.34  If you could walk through the gates and through the towering ramparts
IL.4.35  ὠμὸν βεβρώθοις Πρίαμον Πριάμοιό τε παῖδας
IL.4.35  and eat Priam and the children of Priam raw, and the other
IL.4.36  ἄλλους τε Τρῶας, τότε κεν χόλον ἐξακέσαιο.
IL.4.36  Trojans, then, then only might you glut at last your anger.

More often, however, a speaker refers to a character who is absent but whose fate concerns him in one way or another. For instance, in Book 15 Hera evokes Zeus indirectly, although no less persuasively, to the other gods rather than directly to his face:

IL.15.104  νήπιοι οἳ Ζηνὶ μενεαίνομεν ἀφρονέοντες·
IL.15.104  'Fools, we who try to work against Zeus, thoughtlessly.
IL.15.105  ἢ ἔτι μιν μέμαμεν καταπαυσέμεν ἆσσον ἰόντες
IL.15.105  Still we are thinking in our anger to go near, and stop him
IL.15.106  ἢ ἔπει ἠὲ βίῃ· ὃ δ' ἀφήμενος οὐκ ἀλεγίζει
IL.15.106  by argument or force. He sits apart and cares nothing
IL.15.107  οὐδ' ὄθεται· φησὶν γὰρ ἐν ἀθανάτοισι θεοῖσι
IL.15.107  nor thinks of us, and says that among the other immortals
IL.15.108  κάρτεΐ τε σθένεΐ τε διακριδὸν εἶναι ἄριστος.
IL.15.108  he is pre-eminently the greatest in power and strength.

And in Book 16 Patroclus portrays for Achilles the plight of the Greeks:

IL.16.23  οἳ μὲν γὰρ δὴ πάντες, ὅσοι πάρος ἦσαν ἄριστοι,
IL.16.23  For all those who were before the bravest in battle
IL.16.24  ἐν νηυσὶν κέαται βεβλημένοι οὐτάμενοί τε.
IL.16.24  are lying up among the ships with arrow or spear wounds.

Sometimes a character becomes the spokesman for his own people, as when Hector convinces Paris of the desperate situation of the Trojans by dramatizing it in vivid scenographic detail:

IL.6.325  τὸν δ' Ἕκτωρ νείκεσσεν ἰδὼν αἰσχροῖς ἐπέεσσι:
IL.6.325  But Hector saw him, and in words of shame he rebuked him:
IL.6.326  δαιμόνι' οὐ μὲν καλὰ χόλον τόνδ' ἔνθεο θυμῷ,
IL.6.326  'Strange man! It is not fair to keep in your heart this coldness.
IL.6.327  λαοὶ μὲν φθινύθουσι περὶ πτόλιν αἰπύ τε τεῖχος
IL.6.327  The people are dying around the city and around the steep wall
IL.6.328  μαρνάμενοι: σέο δ' εἵνεκ' ἀϋτή τε πτόλεμός τε
IL.6.328  as they fight hard; and it is for you that this war with its clamour
IL.6.329  ἄστυ τόδ' ἀμφιδέδηε:
IL.6.329  has flared up about our city.

The meaning of such passages is determined not only by the identity of meta-narrator and meta-protagonist, however, but of meta-narratee as well. In the following scene, for example, Dolon is coerced by Odysseus to describe the Trojan camp, information which eventually dooms his own people:

IL.10.418  ὅσσαι μὲν Τρώων πυρὸς ἐσχάραι, οἷσιν ἀνάγκη
IL.10.418  As for the watchfire hearths of the Trojans, those who must do it
IL.10.419  οἳ δ' ἐγρηγόρθασι φυλασσέμεναί τε κέλονται
IL.10.419  keep awake by the fires and pass on the picket duty
IL.10.420  ἀλλήλοις: ἀτὰρ αὖτε πολύκλητοι ἐπίκουροι
IL.10.420  to each other, but their far-assembled companions in battle
IL.10.421  εὕδουσι: Τρωσὶν γὰρ ἐπιτραπέουσι φυλάσσειν:
IL.10.421  are sleeping, and pass on to the Trojans the duty of watching,
IL.10.422  οὐ γάρ σφιν παῖδες σχεδὸν εἴαται οὐδὲ γυναῖκες.
IL.10.422  since their own children do not lie nearby, nor their women.'

Vignette may also bridge the gap between mortal and immortal, as when Zeus evokes Troy (4.34-6) or Apollo Achilles' shelter:

IL.4.509  ὄρνυσθ' ἱππόδαμοι Τρῶες μηδ' εἴκετε χάρμης
IL.4.509  'Rise up, Trojans, breakers of horses, bend not from battle
IL.4.510  Ἀργείοις, ἐπεὶ οὔ σφι λίθος χρὼς οὐδὲ σίδηρος
IL.4.510  with these Argives. Surely their skin is not stone, not iron
IL.4.511  χαλκὸν ἀνασχέσθαι ταμεσίχροα βαλλομένοισιν:

117

IL.4.511 to stand up under the tearing edge of the bronze as it strikes them.

IL.4.512 οὐ μὰν οὐδ' Ἀχιλεὺς Θέτιδος πάϊς ἠϋκόμοιο

IL.4.512 No, nor is Achilles the child of lovely-haired Thetis

IL.4.513 μάρναται, ἀλλ' ἐπὶ νηυσὶ χόλον θυμαλγέα πέσσει.

IL.4.513 fighting, but beside the ship mulls his heartsore anger.'

The most exotic destination for a character's excursion to the Elsewhere, however, is when Achilles evokes, not a specific location, but rather a simile-like forest:

IL.1.234 ναὶ μὰ τόδε σκῆπτρον, τὸ μὲν οὔ ποτε φύλλα καὶ ὄζους

IL.1.234 in the name of this sceptre, which never again will bear leaf nor

IL.1.235 φύσει, ἐπεὶ δὴ πρῶτα τομὴν ἐν ὄρεσσι λέλοιπεν,

IL.1.235 branch, now that it has left behind the cut stump in the mountains,

IL.1.236 οὐδ' ἀναθηλήσει: περὶ γάρ ῥά ἑ χαλκὸς ἔλεψε

IL.1.236 nor shall it ever blossom again, since the bronze blade stripped

IL.1.237 φύλλά τε καὶ φλοιόν: νῦν αὖτέ μιν υἷες Ἀχαιῶν

IL.1.237 bark and leafage, and now at last the sons of the Achaians

IL.1.238 ἐν παλάμαις φορέουσι δικασπόλοι, οἵ τε θέμιστας

IL.1.238 carry it in their hands in state when they administer

IL.1.239 πρὸς Διὸς εἰρύαται: ὃ δέ τοι μέγας ἔσσεται ὅρκος:

IL.1.239 the justice of Zeus. And this shall be a great oath before you:

By doing so, Achilles emulates the omniscient tone of the narrator that is evident, for example, in certain similes, such as this evocation of an isolated olive tree:

IL.17.50 δούπησεν δὲ πεσών, ἀράβησε δὲ τεύχε' ἐπ' αὐτῷ.

IL.17.50 He fell, thunderously, and his armour clattered upon him,

IL.17.51 αἵματί οἱ δεύοντο κόμαι Χαρίτεσσιν ὁμοῖαι

IL.17.51 and his hair, lovely as the Graces, was splattered with blood, those

IL.17.52 πλοχμοί θ', οἳ χρυσῷ τε καὶ ἀργύρῳ ἐσφήκωντο.

IL.17.52 braided locks caught waspwise in gold and silver. As some

IL.17.53 οἷον δὲ τρέφει ἔρνος ἀνὴρ ἐριθηλὲς ἐλαίης

IL.17.53 slip of an olive tree strong-growing that a man raises

IL.17.54 χώρῳ ἐν οἰοπόλῳ, ὅθ' ἅλις ἀναβέβρυχεν ὕδωρ,

IL.17.54 in a lonely place, and drenched it with generous water, so that

IL.17.55 καλὸν τηλεθάον: τὸ δέ τε πνοιαὶ δονέουσι

IL.17.55 it blossoms into beauty, and the blasts of winds from all quarters

IL.17.56 παντοίων ἀνέμων, καί τε βρύει ἄνθεϊ λευκῷ:

IL.17.56 tremble it, and it bursts into pale blossoming.

By employing vignette within similes, the narrator transports the audience to intimate areas of the dramatic landscape, thereby heightening their receptive immediacy and increasing the verisimilitude of the scene. In the following simile, for example, the phrase κεῖται δ' ἐν θαλάμῳ in line 143 vivifies an otherwise routine figurative excursion, achieving what Roland Barthes calls a "reality effect":[213]

IL.4.141  ὡς δ' ὅτε τίς τ' ἐλέφαντα γυνὴ φοίνικι μιήνῃ
IL.4.141  As when some Maionian woman or Karian with purple
IL.4.142  Μῃονὶς ἠὲ Κάειρα παρήϊον ἔμμεναι ἵππων:
IL.4.142  colours ivory, to make it a cheek piece for horses;
IL.4.143  κεῖται δ' ἐν θαλάμῳ, πολέες τέ μιν ἠρήσαντο
IL.4.143  <u>it lies away in an inner room</u>, and many a rider
IL.4.144  ἱππῆες φορέειν: βασιλῆϊ δὲ κεῖται ἄγαλμα,
IL.4.144  longs to have it, but it is laid up to be a king's treasure,
IL.4.145  ἀμφότερον κόσμος θ' ἵππῳ ἐλατῆρί τε κῦδος:
IL.4.145  two things, to be the beauty of the horse, the pride of the horseman:
IL.4.146  τοῖοί τοι Μενέλαε μιάνθην αἵματι μηροὶ
IL.4.146  so, Menelaos, your shapely thighs were stained with the colour
IL.4.147  εὐφυέες κνῆμαί τε ἰδὲ σφυρὰ κάλ' ὑπένερθε.
IL.4.147  of blood, and your legs also and the ankles beneath them.

Likewise, the phrase ἣ μέν τ' ἀζομένη κεῖται ποταμοῖο παρ' ὄχθας in the following evocation of a tree-stump makes a similar appeal to lived experience, without which the simile would merely serve the practical function of establishing the provenience of the chariot-wheel:

IL.4.482  ἦλθεν: ὃ δ' ἐν κονίῃσι χαμαὶ πέσεν αἴγειρος ὣς
IL.4.482  He dropped then to the ground in the dust, like some black poplar,
IL.4.483  ἥ ῥά τ' ἐν είαμενῇ ἕλεος μεγάλοιο πεφύκει
IL.4.483  which in the land low-lying about a great marsh grows
IL.4.484  λείη, ἀτάρ τέ οἱ ὄζοι ἐπ' ἀκροτάτῃ πεφύασι:
IL.4.484  smooth trimmed yet with branches growing at the uttermost tree-top:
IL.4.485  τὴν μέν θ' ἁρματοπηγὸς ἀνὴρ αἴθωνι σιδήρῳ
IL.4.485  one whom a man, a maker of chariots, fells with the shining
IL.4.486  ἐξέταμ', ὄφρα ἴτυν κάμψῃ περικαλλέϊ δίφρῳ:
IL.4.486  iron, to bend it into a wheel for a fine-wrought chariot,
IL.4.487  ἣ μέν τ' ἀζομένη κεῖται ποταμοῖο παρ' ὄχθας.

---

[213] 1989: *passim*.

119

IL.4.487 and the tree lies hardening by the banks of a river.

IL.4.488 τοῖον ἄρ' Ἀνθεμίδην Σιμοείσιον ἐξενάριξεν

IL.4.488 Such was Anthemion's son Simoeisios, whom killed

IL.4.489 Αἴας διογενής:

IL.4.489 illustrious Aias.

This prerogative assumed by Achilles transcends the use that other characters make of vignette and corroborates Griffin's notion of Achilles as the most Elsewhere-preoccupied character in the *Iliad*.[214]

Perhaps the most poignant use of vignette is when a character, whether Greek or Trojan, evokes his own father, as Adrestos and Diomedes do in 6.47-50 and 14.112-14, respectively, or as Achilles brings us once again to Phthia, where he imagines his father suffering vicarious pain for his loss of Patroclus:

IL.19.321 σῇ ποθῇ: οὐ μὲν γάρ τι κακώτερον ἄλλο πάθοιμι,

IL.19.321 of longing for you. There is nothing worse than this I could suffer,

IL.19.322 οὐδ' εἴ κεν τοῦ πατρὸς ἀποφθιμένοιο πυθοίμην,

IL.19.322 not even if I were to hear of the death of my father

IL.19.323 ὅς που νῦν Φθίηφι τέρεν κατὰ δάκρυον εἴβει

IL.19.323 who now, I think, in Phthia somewhere lets fall a soft tear

IL.19.324 χήτεϊ τοιοῦδ' υἷος: ὁ δ' ἀλλοδαπῷ ἐνὶ δήμῳ

IL.19.324 for bereavement of such a son, for me, who now in a strange land

IL.19.325 εἵνεκα ῥιγεδανῆς Ἑλένης Τρωσὶν πολεμίζω:

IL.19.325 make war upon the Trojans for the sake of accursed Helen;

This image of Peleus reflecting upon his son is so powerful that Homer reprises it in Book 24. Only now it is not Achilles himself who imagines his father in Phthia, but rather Priam, who exploits vignette as though aware of its rhetorical potential. Hera he appeals to Achilles' pity by giving him hope that he, unlike his own son, might one day return home to his father:

IL.24.490 ἀλλ' ἤτοι κεῖνός γε σέθεν ζώοντος ἀκούων

IL.24.490 Yet surely he, when he hears of you and that you are still living,

IL.24.491 χαίρει τ' ἐν θυμῷ, ἐπί τ' ἔλπεται ἤματα πάντα

IL.24.491 is gladdened within his heart and all his days he is hopeful

---

[214] 1980: 75, 157; 1986: 53.

IL.24.492   ὄψεσθαι φίλον υἱὸν ἀπὸ Τροίηθεν ἰόντα:
IL.24.492   that he will see his beloved son come home from the Troad.

Thus Homer exploits vignette thematically through the recurrence of Achilles and Peleus within a Phthian context. The most extensive thematic use he makes of the device, however, pertains not to Greek heroes, nor even to Olympian gods, but to a group of characters who otherwise play a relatively minor role in the *Iliad* yet who are nevertheless the most significant protagonists of the Elsewhere: Greek and Trojan women.

The first woman depicted in the *Iliad*, and thus in extant western literature, appears not within the main action but rather in the Elsewhere, through the eyes of Agamemnon, who envisions her in a particularly unflattering light (1.29-31). This overt disrespect towards Briseis, reiterated in lines 112-13, initiates a rhetorical conflict between Agamemnon and Achilles that parallels their more conspicuous disharmony on the level of the story and is not fully resolved until Book 9, after a series of excursions to the Elsewhere charting the progress of this crucial sub-plot. The next vignette featuring female protagonists, and the second stage in the meta-narrative, occurs in Book 2. The meta-narrator is still Agamemnon, who continues to make rhetorical use of the device, only now his intention is not threaten or to frighten but rather to persuade in a more rational manner, trying to convince the Greeks to desert the war and to return home to their wives and children.

IL.2.134   ἐννέα δὴ βεβάασι Διὸς μεγάλου ἐνιαυτοί,
IL.2.134   And now nine years of mighty Zeus have gone by, and the timbers
IL.2.135   καὶ δὴ δοῦρα σέσηπε νεῶν καὶ σπάρτα λέλυνται:
IL.2.135   of our ships have rotted away and the cables are broken
IL.2.136   αἳ δέ που ἡμέτεραί τ' ἄλοχοι καὶ νήπια τέκνα
IL.2.136   and far away our own wives and our young children
IL.2.137   εἵατ' ἐνὶ μεγάροις ποτιδέγμεναι: ἄμμι δὲ ἔργον
IL.2.137   are sitting within our halls and wait for us, while still our work here
IL.2.138   αὕτως ἀκράαντον οὗ εἵνεκα δεῦρ' ἱκόμεσθα.
IL.2.138   stays forever unfinished as it is, for whose sake we came hither.

Despite his generic appeal to ἄλοχοι καὶ νήπια τέκνα rather than to any

121

particular female protagonist, Agamemnon employs the concrete phrase ἐνὶ μεγάροις[215] to situate the scene as vividly, and thus as persuasively, as possible. The next stage in the meta-narrative concerns Agamemnon once again, yet this time not as meta-narrator but rather as meta-narratee. In lines 225-27 of Book 2, Thersites criticizes Agamemnon for taking Odysseus' advice to stay in Troy after the near desertion caused by Zeus' deceptive dream. To drive his point home he argues that Agamemnon is hardly in need of more spoils, given the abundance of bronze and women in his shelter. By doing so, Thersites establishes women as possessions in the pigheaded manner reminiscent of Agamemnon himself.

At this point a clear distinction is established between two diametrically opposite positions adopted towards women within the meta-narrative. The first tendency, illustrated by Agamemnon and Thersites above, contrasts sharply with the favorable depiction of women as symbols of nostalgic yearning, as introduced in the following two scenes. In the first the primary narrator provides the back-story for the absence of Protesilaos from the Trojan war:[216]

IL.2.695  οἳ δ' εἶχον Φυλάκην καὶ Πύρασον ἀνθεμόεντα
IL.2.695  They who held Phylake and Pyrasos of the flowers,
IL.2.698  τῶν αὖ Πρωτεσίλαος ἀρήϊος ἡγεμόνευε
IL.2.698  of these in turn fighting Protesilaos was leader
IL.2.699  ζωὸς ἐών: τότε δ' ἤδη ἔχεν κάτα γαῖα μέλαινα.
IL.2.699  while he lived; but now the black earth had closed him under,
IL.2.700  τοῦ δὲ καὶ ἀμφιδρυφὴς ἄλοχος Φυλάκῃ ἐλέλειπτο
IL.2.700  whose wife, cheeks torn for grief, was left behind in Phylake
IL.2.701  καὶ δόμος ἡμιτελής: τὸν δ' ἔκτανε Δάρδανος ἀνὴρ

---

[215] This construction will be used later in line 435 of Book 18 by Thetis when she appeals to Hephaestus to fashion new armor for Achilles. It is noteworthy that the subject of this excursion to the Elsewhere is Peleus, who plays such a central role in the thematic complex mentioned above.

[216] This passage also represents a special construction in which two distinct regions of the Elsewhere are evoked within a single instance of the device, thereby extending its scenographic scope. In the present case the contrast between the two locations is especially poignant, similar, in fact, to the thematic complex involving Achilles and Peleus mentioned above. For other examples of this variation, see 2.134-38, 6.45-50, 8.22-35, 11.74-83, 13.758-64, 21.114-25, and 22.508-11.

IL.2.701　and a marriage half completed; a Dardanian man had killed him
IL.2.702　νηὸς ἀποθρῴσκοντα πολὺ πρώτιστον Ἀχαιῶν.
IL.2.702　as he leapt from his ship, far the first of all the Achaians.

In the second scene the Trojan version of this sentiment is expressed directly by the hero Lykaon himself, whose nostalgia for home is rendered even more palpable by the strategic architectural detail in line 213:

IL.5.212　Now if ever I win home again and lay eyes once more
IL.5.213　on my country, and my wife, and the great house with the high roof,
IL.5.214　let some stranger straightway cut my head from my shoulders
IL.5.215　if I do not break this bow in my hands and throw it in the shining
IL.5.216　fire, since as a wind and nothing I have taken it with me.'

The scene in Book 6 in which Hector visits his wife Andromache for the last time is frequently noted for the poignancy of its main action. It also features, however, an instance of vignette that is no less crucial to its emotional impact. At this point in the narrative, when Hector approaches his own house in order to locate his wife Andromache, the anticipatory tension is compounded by the adverb αἶψα in line 370 so that, when οὐδ' εὖρ' Ἀνδρομάχην λευκώλενον ἐν μεγάροισιν occurs, we are caught off-guard, left to wonder where in fact Andromache can be. Thus, while excursions to the Elsewhere usually divert the audience's attention from the main action in a purely autonomous capacity, in this case the vignette in lines 372-73 answers a question inspired by the preceding action, generating the dramatic tension that culminates in the tearful reunion between husband and wife in lines 394-406:

IL.6.371　οὐδ' εὖρ' Ἀνδρομάχην λευκώλενον ἐν μεγάροισιν,
IL.6.371　but failed to find in the house Andromache of the white arms;
IL.6.372　ἀλλ' ἥ γε ξὺν παιδὶ καὶ ἀμφιπόλῳ ἐϋπέπλῳ
IL.6.372　for she, with the child, and followed by one fair-robed attendant,
IL.6.373　πύργῳ ἐφεστήκει γοόωσά τε μυρομένη τε.
IL.6.373　had taken her place on the tower in lamentation, and tearful.

In stark contrast with the previous three uses of vignette to portray women as anchors in the emotional life of Protesilaos, Lykaon, and Hector, Book 9 brings us to the final stage of Agamemnon's gradual discomfiture, and the denoument of the meta-narrative. If his previous vision of Briseis slaving away in Argos seemed callous and unsentimental, Agamemnon now attempts to win Achilles back to the Greek cause by sacrificing his own daughters on the altar of political expediency:[217]

IL.9.144 τρεῖς δέ μοί εἰσι θύγατρες ἐνὶ μεγάρῳ εὐπήκτῳ
IL.9.144 Since, as I have three daughters there in my strong-built castle,
IL.9.145 Χρυσόθεμις καὶ Λαοδίκη καὶ Ἰφιάνασσα,
IL.9.145 Chrysothemis and Laodike and Iphianassa,
IL.9.146 τάων ἥν κ' ἐθέλῃσι φίλην ἀνάεδνον ἀγέσθω
IL.9.146 let him lead away the one of these that he likes, with no bride-price,
IL.9.147 πρὸς οἶκον Πηλῆος: ἐγὼ δ' ἐπὶ μείλια δώσω
IL.9.147 to the house of Peleus, and with the girl I will grant him as dowry
IL.9.148 πολλὰ μάλ', ὅσσ' οὔ πώ τις ἑῇ ἐπέδωκε θυγατρί:
IL.9.148 many gifts, such as no man ever gave with his daughter.

Achilles refuses Agamemnon's offer, however, in the most peremptory manner possible: by deflecting his words back at him, evoking the women of Greece as Agamemnon has consistently done up to this point yet to Agamemnon's disadvantage, thereby coopting the Elsewhere as his own rather than Agamemnon's rightful dominion:

IL.9.395 πολλαὶ Ἀχαιίδες εἰσὶν ἀν' Ἑλλάδα τε Φθίην τε
IL.9.395 There are many Achaian girls in the land of Hellas and Phthia,
IL.9.396 κοῦραι ἀριστήων, οἵ τε πτολίεθρα ῥύονται,
IL.9.396 daughters of great men who hold strong places in guard. And of these
IL.9.397 τάων ἥν κ' ἐθέλοιμι φίλην ποιήσομ' ἄκοιτιν.
IL.9.397 any one that I please I might make my beloved lady.
IL.9.398 ἔνθα δέ μοι μάλα πολλὸν ἐπέσσυτο θυμὸς ἀγήνωρ
IL.9.398 And the great desire in my heart drives me rather in that place

---

[217] Agamemnon uses the verb ἀγέσθω in the same emphatic metrical position as Paris and Hector use it in 3.72 and 3.93 in the phrase κτήμαθ' ἑλὼν εὖ πάντα γυναῖκά τε οἴκαδ' ἀγέσθω to refer to Helen and the possessions that will accompany the self-proclaimed κύων either to Greece or Troy, depending upon whether Paris or Menelaos wins their impending duel.

IL.9.399  γήμαντα μνηστὴν ἄλοχον ἐϊκυῖαν ἄκοιτιν
IL.9.399  to take a wedded wife in marriage, the bride of my fancy,
IL.9.400  κτήμασι τέρπεσθαι τὰ γέρων ἐκτήσατο Πηλεύς:
IL.9.400  to enjoy with her the possessions won by aged Peleus.

When Achilles reenters the fray in Book 18, his overt power-struggle with Agamemnon in the Greek camp at the beginning of the *Iliad* seems to be resolved exclusively by his thirst to avenge the death of Patroclus, and thus to depend primarily upon circumstances beyond his control. As we have seen, however, a more subtle, internecine battle has been waged concurrently within the parallel universe of the Elsewhere, throughout the course of a meta-narrative suggesting that, at least in Achilles' mind, the dispute between the two heroes has been fought and won on the battlefield of rhetoric.

# CONCLUSION

"Forces are manifested in poems that do not pass through the circuits of knowledge."
(Bachelard, 1964: xxi)

Homer employs decomposition, intercutting, meta-audience, and vignette in the *Iliad* to promote an interactivity between audience and action whose significance resists structuralist scrutiny. By establishing a tripartite spatial code to represent distances along both the z (decomposition) and x (intercutting) axes of the narrative continuum, Homer creates a sense of inevitability to the way actions are framed from one moment to the next that he may either conform to or diverge from, depending upon the requirements of each individual scene.[218]

He may generate suspense, for example, as to whether the audience will progress from a long shot view of the battlefield to a close-up view of a character upon it or, on the other hand, whether they will maintain throughout the scene a theater-like distance from the action. Likewise, two characters within arrow-shot range of each other may or may not proceed to within spear-shot or sword-stab range of each other, and, if so, with or without tension-building delay-tactics. These are factors that concern the audience, not because of any intrinsic preoccupation with spatiality within the story, but rather because of the systematic way in which Homer frames his audience and characters—and the relationship between them—within narrative space.

Meta-audience and vignette present the *Iliad* through the eyes or the imagination of a given character. By assuming his or her vision the audience in effect becomes a character in their own right, exposed to a visual, and at times emotional, proximity to the action that captivates them in a way otherwise denied to them in their capacity as detached spectators. When they join Andromache in her chamber as the other Trojan women wail outside, her deafness is their deafness, just as her

---

[218] Cf. Pichel, 1970: 113; Landow (1987: 77-8) identifies z- and x-axis motion as the two most characteristic proto-cinematic processes; Feldman (1952: 95) differentiates between decomposition and intercutting based upon conceptual rather than perceptual criteria.

gradual discovery of the truth is also their own. The proximity between regions within Iliadic story space enables Homer to generate suspense about where the audience's attention will be focused next and why. Furthermore, through the constant sense of divine presence in Olympus and on Mount Ida, the gods influence the action even when they do not participate in it directly. When, on the other hand, the action shifts to a region outside of Iliadic story space, it affords temporary refreshment from scenographic monotony. Yet it also reveals a parallel universe where hypothetical scenarios play themselves out in the minds of characters whose actions on the Trojan plain tell only part of the story.

While decomposition, intercutting, meta-audience, and vignette enrich the audience's experience of Homeric epic, however, they generate data that have no bearing, or at most tangential bearing, upon the event-structure of the story. This distinction between events that matter to a narrative and those that do not is a central narratological datum, according to which only bound motifs[219] are significant, precisely because they are essential to the plot, whose constituent events can be isolated and compared with other events both within the story in question and with events from other stories. The result is a methodology that disregards extraneous details, the free motifs generated within narrative space in real time before they are paraphrased into events for subsequent analysis.

In Book 1 of the *Iliad*, for example, the priest Chryses beseeches Apollo to avenge the dishonor he has suffered at the hands of Agamemnon. That is at least the gist of the scene, its event-status from the standpoint of the plot (if, in fact, it can be said to contribute to the plot in the first place[220]). The actual scene, however, is more vital to the audience's experience of the narrative than what an epitome can

---

[219] For the distinction between "bound" and "free" motifs, cf. Prince (1987: 10-11, 36).

[220] In his epitome of the *Iliad* in *A History of Greek Literature* (1996: 24), Lesky omits this scene altogether, as well as the details of Apollo's intervention, presumably because they do not further the story: "[Agamemnon] has incurred Apollo's wrath by failing to restore the captive Chryseis to her father, and the arrows of the god are smiting the host."

convey:[221]

IL.1.34  βῆ δ' ἀκέων παρὰ θῖνα πολυφλοίσβοιο θαλάσσης:
IL.1.34  and went silently away beside the murmuring sea beach.
IL.1.35  πολλὰ δ' ἔπειτ' ἀπάνευθε κιὼν ἠρᾶθ' ὃ γεραιὸς
IL.1.35  Over and over the old man prayed as he walked in solitude
IL.1.36  Ἀπόλλωνι ἄνακτι, τὸν ἠΰκομος τέκε Λητώ:
IL.1.36  to King Apollo, whom Leto of the lovely hair bore:

The image παρὰ θῖνα πολυφλοίσβοιο θαλάσσης (34) presents a pathetic long shot, distancing Chryses from the audience and thereby representing him as a miniscule speck in a vast cosmos, seeking from Apollo a redressing of his grievances toward Agamemnon. When Apollo subsequently plunges vertically from Olympus (44), his actions accentuated by a close-up of the arrows clashing on his shoulders (46), the dramatic effect is heightened by this long shot/close-up perspectival contrast, thereby increasing the tension of the scene.

Because these concerns pertain exclusively to narrative space, however, they are neglected by traditional narratology. Hence Gerard Genette's structuralist interpretation of this passage:

This *shore of the loud-sounding sea* [is] a detail functionally useless in the story...The loud-sounding shore serves no purpose other than to let us understand that the narrative mentions it only because *it is there*, and because the narrator, abdicating his function of choosing and directing the narrative, allows himself to be governed by "reality," by the presence of what is there and what demands to be "shown."[222]

Leonard Lutwack argues, on the other hand, that a poet is not constrained by the sort of "reality" that Genette speaks of, for the verbal medium transcends the scenographic determinism inherent to theater:

There is nothing in the art of narrative that makes place the troublesome problem it is in

---

[221] Cf. Owen (1989), who follows his description of "Chryses praying to Apollo beside the sea," (4) with an admission that "The most interesting feature here...is the immediate introduction of the dramatic method in narrative. We are not so much hearing the story told as seeing it happen," (4-5).
[222] Cf. Kirk (1985: 56).

drama because, being verbalized only, place in narrative cannot have as insistent a presence as it has in stage settings.[223]

As the first extant practitioner of an inherently dynamic art form, Homer exercises the freedom to tailor narrative space to the requirements of each respective epic. In the *Iliad* he constructs a uniform story space and, through the manipulation of discourse spaces within it, maximizes his control over his audience's attention. In the *Odyssey* he subordinates story space to the plot and discourse space to the execution of the plot, until the action shifts to Odysseus' palace, where an *Iliad*–like relationship between audience and action is established. Indeed, narrative space in the *Iliad* and *Odyssey* is more than merely a vehicle to provide scenic backdrops for the action or to increase dramatic verisimilitude: it is the matrix for action itself.

---

[223] 1984: 17.

BIBLIOGRAPHY

Andersen, Oivind. 1990. The Making of the Past in the *Iliad*. Harvard Studies in Classical Philology 93: 25-45.

_____. 1987. Myth, Paradigm and 'Spatial Form' in the *Iliad*. Homer: Beyond Oral Poetry, editors J. M. Bremer, I. J. F. de Jong, and J. Kalff, 1-13. Amsterdam: B.R. Grüner Publishing Co.

Andersson, Theodore M. 1976. Early Epic Scenery: Homer, Virgil, and the Medieval Legacy. Ithaca: Cornell University Press.

Antoniades, Anthony C. 1992. Epic Space: Toward the Roots of Western Architecture. New York: Van Nostrand Reinhold.

Aristotle. 1989. Poetics. Classical Literary Criticism, editors D. A. Russell and M. Winterbottom, 51-90. Oxford: Oxford University Press.

Arnheim, Rudolf. 1957. Film as Art. Berkeley : University of California Press.

_____. 1966. The Gestalt Theory of Expression. Toward a Psychology of Art Rudolf Arnheim, 51-73. Berkeley: University of California Press.

_____. 1987. The Reading of Images and the Images of Reading. Space, Time, Image, Sign: Essays on Literature and the Visual Arts, editor James A.W. Heffernan, 83-8. New York: Peter Lang Publishing, Inc.

_____. 1992. Space as an Image of Time. To the Rescue of Art: Twenty-Six Essays Rudolf Arnheim, 35-44. Berkeley: University of California Press.

_____. 1986. A Stricture on Space and Time. New Essays on the Psychology of Art Rudolf Arnheim, 78-89. Berkeley: University of California Press.

Artaud, Antonin. 1958. The Theater and its Double. New York: Grove Weidenfeld.

Aumont, Jacques and others. 1992. Aesthetics of Film. translator Richard Neupert. Austin: University of Texas Press.

Austin, Norman. 1966. The Function of Digressions in the *Iliad*. Greek, Roman, and Byzantine Studies 7, no. 4: 295-312.

Bachelard, Gaston. 1964. The Poetics of Space. translator Maria Jolas. Boston: Beacon Press.

Bakker, Egbert J. 1993. Discourse and Performance: Involvement, Visualization, and 'Presence' in Homeric Poetry. Classical Antiquity 12, no. 1: 1-29.

_____. 1999. Homeric *houtos* and the Poetics of Deixis. <u>Classical Philology</u> 94: 1-19.

Bal, Mieke. 1985. <u>Narratology: Introduction to the Theory of Narrative</u>. translator Christine van Boheemen. Toronto: University of Toronto Press.

Balutowa, Bronislawa. 1976. Space--Setting--Things in the English Short Story 1900-1925. <u>Kwartalnik Neofilologiczny</u> 23, no. 4: 433-47.

_____. 1979. <u>Spatial Complex: A Study of Spatial Problems in Fiction--Illustrated with Examples from Representative Works of English Short Fiction 1900-1925</u>. Warszawa: Wydawnictwa Uniwersytetu Warszawskiego.

Barthes, Roland. 1989. The Reality Effect. <u>The Rustle of Language</u> Roland Barthes, 141-48. Berkeley: University of California Press.

Bassett, Samuel Eliot. 1938. <u>The Poetry of Homer</u>. Berkeley: University of California Press.

Bassi, Karen. 1998. <u>Acting Like Men: Gender, Drama, and Nostalgia in Ancient Greece</u>. Ann Arbor: University of Michigan Press.

Bazin, André. 1998. The Evolution of the Language of Cinema. <u>Film Theory and Criticism: Introductory Readings</u> Leo Braudy and Marshall Cohen, 43-56. New York: Oxford University Press.

_____. 1998. Theater and Cinema. <u>Film Theory and Criticism: Introductory Readings</u> Leo Braudy and Marshall Cohen, 408-18. New York: Oxford University Press.

_____. 1967. Theater and Cinema--Part One. <u>What is Cinema? Volume 1</u> André Bazin, 76-94. Berkeley: University of California Press.

Becker, Andrew Sprague. 1995. <u>The Shield of Achilles and the Poetics of Ekphrasis</u>. Lanham: Rowman & Littlefield Publishers, Inc.

Benjamin, Walter. 1968. The Work of Art in the Age of Mechanical Reproduction. <u>Illuminations</u> Walter Benjamin, 217-51. New York: Schocken Books.

Bennet, John. 1997. Homer and the Bronze Age. <u>A New Companion to Homer</u>, editors Ian Morris and Barry Powell, 511-34. Leiden: Brill.

Berardinelli, James. The Godfather Part II. 1994. [http://www.reelviews.net].

Bobker, Lee R. 1974. <u>Elements of Film</u>. New York: Harcourt Brace Jovanovich.

Bowra, C. M. 1972. Homer. New York: Scribner.

Braswell, Bruce Karl. 1971. Mythological Innovation in the *Iliad*. The Classical
    Quarterly 65, no. 1: 16-26.

Brecht, Bertolt. 1964. Brecht on Theatre: The Development of an Aesthetic. editor John
    Willett. New York: Hill and Wang.

Brooks, Cleanth. 1974. The Well Wrought Urn: Studies in the Structure of Poetry. San
    Diego: Harcourt Brace & Company.

Browne, Nick. 1999. The Spectator-in-the-Text: The Rhetoric of *Stagecoach*. Film
    Theory and Criticism: Introductory Readings, editors Leo Braudy and Marshall
    Cohen, 148-63. New York: Oxford University Press.

Bryant-Bertail, Sarah. 2000. Space and Time in Epic Theater: The Brechtian Legacy.
    New York: Camden House.

Butler, Bill. 2000. Visions of Light. directors Arnold Glassman and Stuart Samuels.

Carter, Jane B. 1995. Ancestor Cult and the Occasion of Homeric Performance. Jane B.
    Carter and Sarah P. Morris, 285-312. Austin: University of Texas.

Cassirer, Ernst. 1946. Language and Myth. translator Susanne K. Langer. New York:
    Dover Publications, Inc.

Chatman, Seymour. 1981. Reply to Barbara Herrnstein Smith. On Narrative, editor W. J.
    T. Mitchell, 258-65. Chicago: University of Chicago Press.

————. 1978. Story and Discourse: Narrative Structure in Fiction and Film. Ithaca:
    Cornell University Press.

————. 1981. What Novels Can Do That Films Can't (and Vice Versa). editor W. J.
    T. Mitchell, 117-36. Chicago: University of Chicago Press.

Columbia Electronic Encyclopedia. Cartesian coordinates, Mathematics. 2003.
    [http://reference.allrefer.com/encyclopedia/C/Cartes-coo.html].

Cortex. SLC Punk! 2002. [http://www.imdb.com].

Culler, Jonathan. 1986. Ferdinand de Saussure. Ithaca: Cornell University Press.

Davis, Ellen N. 1991. The Iconography of the Ship Fresco from Thera. Looking at Greek
    Vases, editors Tom Rasmussen and Nigel Spivey, 3-14. Cambridge: Cambridge
    University Press.

Davis, Lennard J. 1986. 'Known Unknown' Locations: The Ideology of Novelistic Landscape in Robinson Crusoe. Sociocriticism 4/5: 87-113.

de Certeau, Michel. 1984. The Practice of Everyday Life. translator Steven Rendall. Berkeley: University of California Press.

de Jong, I. J. F. 1987. Silent Characters in the Iliad. Homer: Beyond Oral Poetry, editors J. M. Bremer, I. J. F. de Jong, and J. Kalff, 105-21. Amsterdam: B.R. Grüner Publishing Co.

Demont, Paul and Anne Lebeau. 1996. Introduction au théâtre grec antique. Paris: Le Livre de Poche.

Dirks, Tim. A Clockwork Orange. 1996. [http://www.filmsite.org].

Dmytryk, Edward. 1988. Cinema: Concept and Practice. Boston: Focal Press.

Dodds, E. R. 1951. The Greeks and the Irrational. Berkeley: University of California Press.

Duckworth, Colin. 1990. From Stage Space to Inner Space in Beckett's Drama: Signposts to Elsewhere. Space and Boundaries in Literature, editor Roger Bauer, 131-37. München: Iudicium Verlag.

Eades, Caroline and Françoise Létoublon. 1999. From Film Analysis to Oral-Formulaic Theory: The Case of the Yellow Oilskins. Contextualizing Classics: Ideology, Performance, Dialogue, editors Thomas M. Falkner, Nancy Felson, and David Konstan, 301-16. Lanham: Rowman & Littlefield Publishers, Inc.

Ebert, Roger. The Dancer Upstairs. 2003. [http://www.suntimes.com].

Ebert, Roger. Elephant. 2003. [http://www.suntimes.com].

Ebert, Roger. Patton. 2002. [http://www.suntimes.com].

Ebert, Roger. Troy. 2004. [http://www.suntimes.com].

Edmunds, Lowell. 1996. Theatrical Space and Historical Place in Sophocles' Oedipus at Colonus. Lanham: Rowman & Littlefield Publishers, Inc.

Edwards, Mark W. 1987. Homer: Poet of the Iliad. Baltimore/London: Johns Hopkins University Press.

Eisenstein, Sergei. 1970. The Dynamic Square. Film Essays and a Lecture Sergei Eisenstein, 48-65. New York: Praeger Publishers.

_____. 1977. Film Form: Essays in Film Theory. San Diego: Harcourt Brace and Company.

_____. 1970. Lessons from Literature. Film Essays and a Lecture Sergei Eisenstein, 77-84. New York: Praeger Publishers.

Eliade, Mircea. 1959. The Sacred and the Profane: The Nature of Religion. translator Willard R. Trask. San Diego: Harcourt Brace and Company.

Else, Gerald F. 1965. The Origin and Early Form of Greek Tragedy. Cambridge: Harvard University Press.

Esrock, Ellen Joann. 1987. Response to Rudolf Arnheim. Space, Time, Image, Sign: Essays on Literature and the Visual Arts, editor James A. W. Heffernan, 88-91. New York: Peter Lang Publishing, Inc.

Esslin, Martin. 1976. An Anatomy of Drama. New York: Hill and Wang.

Feldman, Joseph and Harry Feldman. 1952. Dynamics of the Film. New York: Hermitage House, Inc.

Fell, John L. 1975. Film: An Introduction. New York: Praeger Publishers.

Fischer-Lichte, Erika. 1992. The Semiotics of Theater. translators Jeremy Gaines and Doris L. Jones. Bloomington/Indianapolis: Indiana University Press.

Fish, Stanley E. 1980. Interpreting the Variorum. Reader-Response Criticism: From Formalism to Post-Structuralism, editor Jane P. Tompkins, 164-84. Baltimore: Johns Hopkins University Press.

_____. 1980. Literature in the Reader: Affective Stylistics. Reader-Response Criticism: From Formalism to Post-Structuralism, editor Jane P. Tompkins, 70-100. Baltimore: Johns Hopkins University Press.

Foley, John Miles. 1999. Homer's Traditional Art. University Park: Pennsylvania State University Press.

Foucault, Michel. 1970. The Order of Things: An Archaeology of the Human Sciences. New York: Vintage Books.

Frazier, Melissa. 1999. Space and Genre in Gogol's Arabeski. Slavic and East European Journal 43, no. 3: 452-70.

Genette, Gérard. 1980. Narrative Discourse: An Essay in Method. translator Jane E. Lewin. Ithaca: Cornell University Press.

135

Gentili, Bruno. 1988. Poetry and Its Public in Ancient Greece: From Homer to the Fifth Century. Baltimore: Johns Hopkins University Press.

Gillespie, Stuart. 1988. Homer. The Poets on the Classics: An Anthology of English Poets' Writings on the Classical Poets and Dramatists from Chaucer to the Present Stuart Gillespie, 95-115. London/New York: Routledge.

Goffman, Erving. 1974. Frame Analysis: An Essay on the Organization of Experience. Boston: Northeastern University Press.

Green, J. R. 1994. Theatre in Ancient Greek Society. London: Routledge.

Greimas, A. J. 1990. The Social Sciences: A Semiotic View. translators P. Perron and F. H. Collins. Minneapolis: University of Minnesota Press.

Griffin, Jasper. 1978. The Divine Audience and the Religion of the *Iliad*. The Classical Quarterly 28: 1-22.

_____. 1980. Homer on Life and Death. Oxford: Clarendon Press.

Griffith, L. A. 1925. When the Movies Were Young. New York: E.P. Dutton and Company.

Gülich, Elisabeth and Uta M. Quasthoff. 1985. Narrative Analysis. Handbook of Discourse Analysis: Dimensions of Discourse (Volume 2), editor Teun A. van Dijk, 169-97. Orlando: Academic Press, Inc.

Hainsworth, Bryan. 1993. The Iliad: A Commentary, Volume 3: Books 9-12. Cambridge: Cambridge University Press.

Havelock, Eric A. 1987. Some Elements of the Homeric Fantasy. Homer's The Iliad, editor Harold Bloom, 93-109. New York: Chelsea House.

Hawkes, Terence. 1977. Structuralism and Semiotics. Berkeley: University of California Press.

Heath, Malcolm. 1987. The Poetics of Greek Tragedy. London: Duckworth.

Heffernan, James A. W. 1987. Space and Time in Literature and the Visual Arts. Soundings 70, no. 1-2: 95-119.

_____. 1987. The Temporalization of Space in Wordsworth, Turner, and Constable. Space, Time, Image, Sign: Essays on Literature and the Visual Arts, editor James A. W. Heffernan, 63-77. New York: Peter Lang Publishing, Inc.

Hellwig, Brigitte. 1964. Raum und Zeit im homerischen Epos. Hildesheim: Georg Olms.

Hiller, S. 1983. Discussion (after "Steps Toward Representational Art in 8th-Century Vase Painting" by J. Schäfer, pp. 75-81). The Greek Renaissance of the Eighth Century B.C.: Tradition and Innovation, Haäg, Robin, 81-2. Stockholm: Svenska Institutet i Athen.

Horrocks, Geoffrey C. 1981. Space and Time in Homer: Prepositional and Adverbial Particles in the Greek Epic. New York: Arno Press.

Hurwit, Jeffrey. 1977. Image and Frame in Greek Art. American Journal of Archaeology: 1-30.

Iser, Wolfgang. 1980. The Reading Process: A Phenomenological Approach. Reader-Response Criticism: From Formalism to Post-Structuralism, editor Jane P. Tompkins, 50-69. Baltimore: Johns Hopkins University Press.

Issacharoff, Michael. 1981. Space and Reference in Drama. Poetics Today 2, no. 3: 211-24.

Jones, P. V. 1992. The Past in Homer's Odyssey. Journal of Hellenic Studies 112: 74-90.

Kahane, Ahuvia and Martin Mueller. 2001. The Chicago Homer Project: An Electronic Database Tool for the Study of Early Epic. Chicago: University of Chicago Press.

Kauffmann, Stanley. 1974. Notes on Theater-and-Film. Focus on Film and Theater, editor James Hurt, 67-77. New York: Prentice-Hall.

Kepley, Vance, Jr. 1995. Pudovkin and the Continuity Style: Problems of Space and Narration. Discourse 17, no. 3: 85-100.

Kirk, G. S. 1985. The Iliad: A Commentary, Volume 1: Books 1-4. Cambridge: Cambridge University Press.

Klein, Holger M. 1990. Exploring Place and Space in Drama and in Fiction. Space and Boundaries in Literature, editor Roger Bauer, 174-81. München: Iudicium Verlag.

Kuntz, Mary. 1993. Narrative Setting and Dramatic Poetry. Leiden/New York/Köln: E.J. Brill.

Landow, George P. 1987. Response to James A.W. Heffernan. Space, Time, Image, Sign: Essays on Literature and the Visual Arts, editor James A. W. Heffernan, 77-81. New York : Peter Lang Publishing, Inc.

137

Langellier, Kristin M. 1981. The Semiotic Function of Audience. Semiotics: 107-16.

Lateiner, Donald. 1995. Sardonic Smile: Nonverbal Behavior in Homeric Epic. Ann
Arbor: University of Michigan Press.

Leach, Eleanor Winsor. 2000. Narrative Space and the Viewer in Philostratus' *Eikones*.
Mitteilungen Des Deutschen Arch. Inst. Rom. Abt 107: 237-51.

_____. 1988. The Rhetoric of Space: Literary and Artistic Representations of
Landscape in Republican and Augustan Rome. Princeton: Princeton University
Press.

Lesky, Albin. 1996. A History of Greek Literature. translators Cornelis de Heer and
James Willis. Indianapolis: Hackett Publishing Company.

Lessing, Gotthold Ephraim. 1984. Laocoön: An Essay on the Limits of Painting and
Poetry. translator Edward Allen McCormick. Baltimore: Johns Hopkins
University Press.

Lieblein, Leanore. 1986. Green Plots and Hawthorn Brakes: Towards a Definition of
Performance Space in the Renaissance. Comparative Critical Approaches to
Renaissance Comedy, editors Donald Beecher and Massimo Ciavolella, 119-
26. Ottawa: Dovehouse Editions.

Limon, Jerzy. 1999. From Liturgy to the Globe: The Changing Concept of Space.
Shakespeare Survey: An Annual Survey of Shakespeare Studies and
Production, editor Stanley Wells. Shakespeare and the Globe ed., 46-53.
Cambridge: Cambridge University Press.

Longinus. 1989. On Sublimity. Classical Literary Criticism, editors D. A. Russell and M.
Winterbottom, 143-87. Oxford: Oxford University Press.

Longman, Stanley Vincent. 1987. Fixed, Floating and Fluid Stages. Themes in Drama 9:
The Theatrical Space James Redmond, 151-60. Cambridge: Cambridge
University Press.

Lotman, Jurij. 1976. Semiotics of Cinema. translator Mark E. Suino. Ann Arbor:
University of Michigan.

Lowe, N. J. 2000. The Classical Plot and the Invention of Western Narrative. Cambridge:
Cambridge University Press.

Lutwack, Leonard. 1984. The Role of Place in Literature. Syracuse: Syracuse University
Press.

138

Lyons, John D. 1991. Unseen Space and Theatrical Narrative: The "Récit de Cinna". Yale French Studies 80: 70-90.

Léger, Fernand. 1988. Painting and Cinema. French Film Theory and Criticism: A History/Anthology 1907-1939, editor Richard Abel, 372-73. Princeton: Princeton University Press.

Lévi-Strauss, Claude. 1976. Reflections on a Work by Vladimir Propp. Structural Anthropology, Volume 2 Claude Lévi-Strauss, 115-45University of Chicago Press.

————. 1963. Structural Analysis in Linguistics and in Anthropology. Structural Anthropology Claude Lévi-Strauss, 31-54HarperCollins Publishers .

Marinatos, Nanno. 1984. Art and Religion in Thera: Reconstructing a Bronze Age Society. Athens: D. & I. Mathioulakis.

Martin, Wallace. 1986. Recent Theories of Narrative. Ithaca: Cornell University Press.

Morris, Sarah P. 1989. A Tale of Two Cities: The Miniature Frescoes from Thera and the Origins of Greek Poetry. American Journal of Archaeology 93: 511-35.

Münsterberg, Hugo. 1970. The Film: A Psychological Study. New York: Dover Publications, Inc.

Nicolaescu, Madalina. 1988. Theatrical Space: The Relationship between the Fictional World, the Acting Area and Space of the Spectators. Synthesis 15: 57-62.

Osadnik, Waclaw M. 1994. Some Remarks on the Nature and Representation of Space and Time in Verbal Art, Theatre and Cinema. S 6, no. 1/2: 211-28.

Owen, E. T. 1989. The Story of the Iliad. Bristol: Bristol Classical Press.

Panofsky, Erwin. 1998. Style and Medium in the Motion Pictures. Film Theory and Criticism: Introductory Readings Leo Braudy and Marshall Cohen, 279-92. New York: Oxford University Press.

Perez, Gilberto. 1998. The Material Ghost: Films and their Medium. Baltimore: Johns Hopkins University Press.

Phillips, William H. 1999. Film: An Introduction. Boston: Bedford/St. Martin's.

Pichel, Irving. 1970. Change of Camera Viewpoint. The Movies as Medium, editor Lewis Jacobs, 113-23. New York: Farrar, Straus & Giroux.

Poulet, Georges. 1977. Proustian Space. translator Elliott Coleman. Baltimore: Johns Hopkins University Press.

Prince, Gerald. 1987. A Dictionary of Narratology. Lincoln: University of Nebraska Press.

Pudovkin, V. I. 1960. Film Technique and Film Acting. translator Ivor Montagu. New York: Grove Press, Inc.

Redfield, James M. 1975. Nature and Culture in the Iliad: The Tragedy of Hector . Durham: Duke University Press.

Rehm, Rush. 1994. Greek Tragic Theatre. London: Routledge.

Richardson, Scott. 1990. The Homeric Narrator. Nashville: Vanderbilt University Press.

Ricoeur, Paul. 1981. Narrative Time. On Narrative, editor W. J. T. Mitchell, 165-86. Chicago: University of Chicago Press.

Rieu, E. V. 1950. Homer: The Iliad. New York: Penguin Books.

Rimmon-Kenan, Shlomith. 1983. Narrative Fiction: Contemporary Poetics. London: Routledge.

Romm, James S. 1992. The Edges of the Earth in Ancient Thought: Geography, Exploration, and Fiction. Princeton: Princeton University Press.

Ronen, Ruth. 1990. Places in Allegorical Worlds. Space and Boundaries in Literature, editor Roger Bauer, 32-7. München: Iudicium Verlag.

Schapiro, Meyer. 1969. On Some Problems in the Semiotics of Visual Art: Field and Vehicle in Image-Signs. Semiotica 1, no. 3: 223-42.

Scholes, Robert. 1982. Semiotics and Interpretation. New Haven: Yale University Press.

_____. 1974. Structuralism in Literature: An Introduction. New Haven: Yale University Press.

Scolnicov, Hanna. 1987. Theatre Space, Theatrical Space, and the Theatrical Space Within. Themes in Drama 9: The Theatrical Space, editor James Redmond, 11-26. Cambridge: Cambridge University Press.

Scott, A. O. Signs. 2002. [http://www.newyorktimes.com].

Shklovsky, Viktor. 1990. Theory of Prose. Dalkey Archive Press.

Silk, Michael. 1987. _Homer: The Iliad_. Cambridge: Cambridge University Press.

Singor, H. W. 1995. ENI PRÔTOISI MACHESTHAI: Some Remarks on the Iliadic Image of the Battlefield. _Homeric Questions: Essays in Philology, Ancient History and Archaeology, Including the Papers of a Conference Organized by the Netherlands Institute at Athens (15 May 1993)_, editor Jan Paul Crielaard. Amsterdam: J.C. Gieben.

Smith, Barbara Herrnstein. 1981. Narrative Versions, Narrative Theories. _On Narrative_, editor W. J. T. Mitchell, 209-32. Chicago: University of Chicago Press.

Stansbury-O'Donnell, Mark D. 1999. _Pictorial Narrative in Ancient Greek Art_. Cambridge: Cambridge University Press.

Stern, Seymour. 1979. The Birth of a Nation: The Technique and Its Influence. _The Emergence of Film Art: The Evolution and Development of the Motion Picture as an Art, from 1900 to the Present_ Lewis Jacobs, 58-79. New York: W.W. Norton & Company.

Styan, J. L. 1988. Stage Space and the Shakespeare Experience. _Shakespeare and the Sense of Performance_, editors Marvin Thompson and Ruth Thompson, 195-209. Newark: University of Delaware Press.

Suvin, Darko. 1987. Approach to Topoanalysis and to the Paradigmatics of Dramaturgic Space. _Poetics Today_ 8, no. 2: 311-34.

Todorov, Tzvetan. 1977. _The Poetics of Prose_. translator Richard Howard. Ithaca: Cornell University Press.

Tomkins, Jane P. 1980. _Reader-Response Criticism: From Formalism to Post-Structuralism_. Baltimore: Johns Hopkins University Press.

Vivante, Paolo. 1985. _Homer_. New Haven: Yale University Press.

_____. 1970. _The Homeric Imagination: A Study of Homer's Poetic Perception of Reality_. Bloomington/London: Indiana University Press.

_____. 1995. _The Iliad: Action as Poetry_. New York: Twayne Publishers.

Werth, Paul. 1995. 'World enough, and time': Deictic space and the interpretation of prose. _Twentieth-Century Fiction: From Text to Context_, editors Peter Verdonk and Jean Jacques Weber, 181-205. London/New York: Routledge.

West, M. L. 1981. The Singing of Homer and the Modes of Early Greek Music. _The Journal of Hellenic Studies_ 101: 113-29.

Wiles, David. 1997. <u>Tragedy in Athens: Performance Space and Theatrical Meaning</u>. Cambridge: Cambridge University Press.

Wood, Robert E. 1987. Space and Scrutiny in *Hamlet*. <u>South Atlantic Review</u> 52, no. 1: 25-42.

Wright, M. R. 1995. <u>Cosmology in Antiquity</u>. London: Routledge.

Youngblood, Gene. 2001. <u>L'Avventura</u>, Criterion Collection.

Zoran, Gabriel. 1984. Towards a Theory of Space in Narrative. <u>Poetics Today</u> 5, no. 2: 309-35.

Zsigmond, Vilmos. 2000. <u>Visions of Light</u>. directors Arnold Glassman and Stuart Samuels.

Zweig, Stefan. 1930. <u>Three Masters: Balzac, Dickens, Dostoyevsky</u>. New York: Viking Press.

# ABOUT THE AUTHOR

 Brett Robbins earned his Ph.D. in Classical Studies at Indiana University, Bloomington (dissertation [2004]: *Framing Achilles: Narrative Space in the Iliad*), and his B.A. and M.A. in Classics at University of California, Santa Barbara. He has traveled extensively, e.g., visiting over 100 ancient Greek sites with the American School of Classical Studies at Athens, delivering talks onsite at the Temple of Zeus at Olympia and the Theater of Epidaurus. He joined the Department of Classics and Humanities at San Diego State University in 2005, where he teaches courses in ancient Greek and Latin languages, myth, culture, etymology, drama, and cinema.

CPSIA information can be obtained
at www.ICGtesting.com
Printed in the USA
FSHW021406110122
87570FS

9 780692 828861